ROCK 'N SOUL TAROT

Interpreting the Cards through the Universal
Language of Music

Brian Orlando

Aurora Corialis Publishing

Pittsburgh, PA

Printed in the United States of America
Preliminary Editor: Jamie Lynn Ryan
Copyeditor: Val Brkich, Aurora Corialis Publishing
Cover Design: Karen Captline, BetterBe Creative
Paperback ISBN: 978-1-958481-52-3
Ebook ISBN: 978-1-958481-53-0

Table of Contents

Foreword

(Don't Skip This!)

By Dave "Snake" Sabo, Skid Row

I moved from Los Angeles to Long Island in the summer of 2012. I didn't really know anybody except my soon-to-be wife and some of her friends. One of the first people I met was Brian. I'm not sure where or how. I just knew that there was something about him that I liked. He seemed genuine. And, coming from LA, that was something I hadn't experienced much of in my time there. It felt good to be back on the East Coast.

Orlando, as he introduced himself, had no airs about him. He spoke straight up and honestly, yet humbly, with no pretense or attitude. I found myself thinking that if everyone out here is like this guy, then there are a lot of great people here. Well, there are a lot of great people here, but none like Orlando.

What I heard on the radio was the same guy who I met and had many great conversations with. And I learned that he has what a lot of people strive for: spirit. He wears his heart openly, whether it's talking about Springsteen, the Rangers, his mom, or the path he continues to forge—it's all genuine and honest. I admire the work he does for various charities here on Long Island and the love he has for the community.

His passion and smile are infectious, and regardless of the subject matter and whether you agree or disagree, he will listen even more than he will opine. That's a trait that we sorely need in this world today.

When I was made aware that he could communicate with spirits, I must admit I was surprised—for about ten seconds! And then it made complete sense.

The guy that l have come to know and call a friend has all the markings of someone unique and special, someone who humbly accepts a gift he was born with and chooses to utilize it for the good of others, because that's just who he is. He puts other people's well-being before his own because he believes that his work will help those around him find peace and happiness and, if needed, closure... and that's what gives him the biggest smile on the Island!

I'm proud of Orlando for many reasons, but mostly because he's one of the truly good guys, and we could benefit from more like him.

Prologue

By Vinnie Dombroski, Sponge

To chronicle one's life is an impressive task. To chronicle one's life in the music business, for most, is an easy one. For those on the radio side of things or the music maker side of things, it can all be so short-lived.

If anybody told me 45 years ago that in 2025 I would have some kind of career in the biz, that person would've heard me yell, "You must be high as shit!" In the ever-changing landscape of rock radio, the prediction of Orlando's extended tenure would have been as crazy as someone telling moonshine runner Junior Johnson that he would someday be in the NASCAR Hall of Fame.

So let's talk about what makes folks take a deep dive into the music game—love. The love of music and everything that surrounds it makes the insane hours, the insane demands, and the compromising of your body, mind, and soul acceptable. Being on-air is just a part of the demands of a rock and roll DJ.

The idea of the "end game" was never a question. And—boom!—miraculously, the bills start to take care of themselves. You make it this far in the game, you have no more questions. Just answers. Stories. A book. The answers in Orlando's book.

You don't exist in rock and roll radio without BIG stories to tell. Stories from the love—the love of the ride and the adventure. The love of songs that are deeply personal to him, and the folks that make 'em.

Dig into the book. Hold on to your hat for the ride.

Intro

So, how the fuck did we get here?

When was the last time you actually had a vision of how it was supposed to be? We've all dreamed up different scenarios of how it would all look at different stages in our lives. When we were young, we envisioned our dream professions. As teens, we may have pictured the perfect girlfriend or boyfriend, or a world where it was illegal for parents to impose a curfew. As we reached our 20s, we started to realize that those ideas we had as kids about how it would be when we were adults were a little impractical, perhaps somewhat out of reach. But let me ask you something ... did that ever stop you from dreaming again? Did not getting what you wanted ever stop you from *wanting*?

Now, if you continue to dream, and these aspirations are still dangling out of reach, then I ask you: why? What is it about others who seemingly make up a goal overnight and achieve it six ways from Sunday by the following Saturday, while you still sit there and wonder *why not me?*

Now, I have never been, and don't pretend to be, a Reiki practitioner. I can't sit here and tell you what chakras are blocked and what your inner child is feeling. I doubt your inner child would appreciate my language. But what I can tell you is, whatever is causing you to repeat the same mistakes, conjure up the same limiting beliefs, and fuck up the best things in your life like it's your job, can be stopped. These patterns can be changed, and the good news is, you can start today. The bad news is, it's probably gonna hurt a bit—and you already know that, which is why tomorrow becomes yesterday before today is finished.

We tend to finally push for change when the current situation starts to hurt more than the possibility of improving it, but since that instruction manual on life is still in the mail, this is where we tend to get confused. This is when it's best to talk to someone. Some talk to priests. Some to therapists. Some to their bartender... and why not? The bartender is probably hot.

But there is one person you probably didn't think to ask when it comes to raising your vibration, which is a fancy way of saying to stop living below your potential. Who haven't you asked yet? No, not your parents. They did enough damage. I'm talking about *you*. When was the last time *you* asked yourself why *you* keep fucking up over and over again? Why *you* keep getting passed up for raises while the dickhead who just got to the company last week already has an office and expense account? Why haven't *you* asked *YOU* why every relationship you're in could be the inspiration for *Fatal Attraction 2*?

Now, the easy answer is because you're the one who keeps making these bad decisions, so how would you know what the answer is? Well, that's easy. You're asking the wrong *you*. Your current self has no fucking idea why you're a mess. But your higher self... your higher self knows why *and* knows how to change how you think, so this whole 'life' thing becomes more fulfilling.

Okay, so what the fuck is my "higher self," and is he on Facebook?

Your higher self is with you right now. But as we grew older, we got jaded and the weather stripped away the glow, so that higher self has been curled up deep within you. But it's still there. You just have to stop moving, stop shouting and fucking listen.

That's where Tarot comes in. This is where intuitive guidance is most valuable and can make a major difference in what you see, feel, gain, and experience. The answers are deep inside that crusty soul of yours. And with a little bit of discipline, determination, and a check of the ego, that deck of Tarot that you purchased can help you unlock these answers, and more importantly, unlock the right questions to ask. Once you accept that your intuitive self can help that stubborn—and sometimes annoying—present self, you are more than on your way to breaking bad habits, making more grounded decisions, and even feeling better.

So, you may be asking, how the fuck do I start? I'm supposed to memorize seventy-eight card meanings and reversals, and just like that, life is gonna magically improve? No. Remember the part where we said it's gonna hurt a little? Anything new can be scary, but when you make it fun and relatable, the ride is a lot more comfortable.

I grew up around Tarot cards and astrologers and psychic mediums. These people were in my life since I was three years old because my mom read Tarot professionally to help keep the lights on. Since as long as I can remember, I'd be in someone's kitchen playing with my GI Joes while a line of people waited to be read by my mother in the next room, or random people would be waiting on my couch telling me how amazing my mother was and how excited they were to be getting a reading. As I got older, my friends would even ask if my mother could throw a few cards out for them.

So, this is probably where you would think my journey with Tarot began, right? I couldn't fucking stand this stuff. My mother is great? Have you tried her pot roast? Wait, why are you in my home? You don't know if you're in the right relationship? Okay, see a therapist and let me go back to watching *DuckTales*, you weirdo.

There is also a dark side to intuitive guidance that turned me off more than my mother's practice and her merry band of witchy friends: the addictive nature of it... of not making a single decision without asking your psychic or pulling a card. You know that the present you—the one who keeps fucking up—YOU can make some decent decisions, and there is a time when *that* you needs to act. The trick is to open up to where your higher self is constantly guiding your present self, and you have enough trust in you and the universe, so that whatever move you make is with enough confidence that it's all gonna be alright.

Too many nights, I've seen my mom sitting Indian style on the floor with the cards spread all around her, asking whatever question was on her mind that day, instead of going out and getting the answer. This, and a few things my therapist and I have gone over, is why it took me forty-one years to finally embrace this side of me. So, I get how scary it can be. I understand how jaded you might be toward the idea of allowing Tarot and intuitive guidance into your life.

We just met, so I don't expect you to just trust me. I am gonna make it as cool of an experience as possible and hope that what's helped me embrace this wacky world will also help you find your own way within it.

As you might have picked up on, this is not a traditional book on Tarot full of clichéd terminology and flowery bullshit. Oh, child, there is such abundance in your life. Sure there is. If you put in the fucking work. So, how are we going to learn together so that you can do the work on your own, with help from your higher self and a few friends watching over you along the way? By learning Tarot through the one language I am confident I understand: **rock and roll.** The genre of music that has ALWAYS been questioned, misunderstood, and criticized for not fitting into mainstream norms.

I'm a radio DJ. Remember when we talked at the beginning of this intro about picturing what your life would be like when you were a kid? Yeah, I never thought I'd be a radio DJ or a Tarot card reader. I was going to be a WWF wrestler. When I wasn't in the ring, I would be on stage singing with my world-renowned rock band because music has always been my saving grace. My guide. When nothing made sense, the right song always found me to remind me I wasn't alone.

At fifteen, when I foolishly tried to take my own life, it was music that snapped me out of it. When I navigated through two failed marriages, it was music that made me feel better. When I finally became the morning show radio host of my hometown rock station, it was because of music and my love for it. So, music is how we are going to learn Tarot together. And what I've learned throughout these forty-six years as a DJ, promoter, event organizer, and son of a psychic will help me help you become your own version of an intuitive guide—to help not just you, but anyone who you allow to seek your guidance.

Music is the one thing that always made me feel like I was never alone. There is a song for every emotion we feel. Just like there is a Tarot card or two that represents that emotion. There is a song for every type of breakup. Tarot has a few cards for them. The Tower, the Three of Swords. There are songs that remind you that it's been too long since you saw your friends, like "Blood on Blood" by Bon Jovi and "Bobby Jean" by Bruce Springsteen. The Six of Cups and the Three of Wands can have you picking up the phone just as quickly. So... are you ready to begin?

Let's rock!

Major Arcana

o • The Fool

Many Tarot card booklets and instructional novels about how to read your deck discuss The Fool in an almost romantic light. This idea of leaping before you look, directly into the wind without a care in the world, just to see where you land, *seems* like it could be fun—but let's ask a few questions first.

WHY is he taking a blind leap?

WHAT exactly is he leaving behind?

When we ask anyone for advice, there's usually something going on. No one sits before a psychic and says, "Everything is great right now. What can you tell me?"

In the case of The Fool, you are leaving *everything* you know behind to start over, and you don't even know where or when that will be. If I said to you, "I'm just gonna drive my car until I run out of gas, and wherever I wind up when the gas tank is empty is where my new life will be. Tell my family and my job I said what's up..." *What would you tell me?* There is a reason why they call him The FOOL.

Can you think of any reasons, off the top of your head, as to why you would leave it all behind without looking back? Do any of them sound pleasant?

Even the most positive situations can be risky, like...say you're planning on leaving a position you have been at for twenty years to finally work at your dream job, which may sound great, but you start tomorrow, and your dream position is in Delaware, and you live on Long Island. So, the anxiety and the pressure of a life-changing decision are still weighing on you.

The song that always makes me think of The Fool is "Runaway Train" by Soul Asylum. It might have been one of the biggest hits of 1993, and for an angry fifteen-year-old who didn't fit in anywhere, that song was everything. Throughout the song's four minutes, lead singer Dave Pirner paints a picture of boredom, despair, and the frustration of not being able to get anything going in his life. The narrator of the song expresses his desperation to be turned like a key and connected with in any way possible, but the stagnation of his life has left him exhausted, yet too sad to sleep.

What always chilled me to the bone, even with only a decade and a half of experience on the earth in 1993, is at the bridge, where he talks about laughing into the rain as a metaphor for his plan of leaving it all behind. It might seem crazy, but he has nothing else to hope for. So even though the risk is astronomical, the thought of staying where he is seems worse. When The Fool shows up, there is a reason to leave it all behind. What are some situations that might make you feel this way?

In 2004, I had zero direction. I was twenty-six and had already attended more funerals for friends than my parents had for theirs. I had been laid off from my truck driver's job delivering food to schools, which I thought, I was *told*, was only for the summer. September came, and so did paperwork for unemployment benefits, and my boss never picked up the phone again. My landlord wanted to give my apartment to his family, and between being homeless, jobless, and many of my friends not being around anymore, I had a breakdown. I lost it.

My mother and I never had a great relationship, but as I stood there screaming in the parking lot of her apartment complex, I wanted to crumble. I wanted to be taken away and never to be seen again. Instead, I wound up in jail for a night, I still had to face this mess I called a life, and now I had to face a judge as well. Looking around the town I grew up in, I barely recognized it.

Looking back, I can tell you it was my eyes that were cloudy, but I knew I needed to get away. With no job, no place to live, and no confidence, I got into my car and drove 250 miles to South Jersey. I had some family and a girlfriend there. Yes, I was dating a girl in another state at the time. None of my decisions made sense, but here I was, headed over a few bridges to start a new life.

Before I even started the car, I made sure "Runaway Train" was in my CD player. This move would lead me to my career in radio, and I would get to tell Dave Pirner of Soul Asylum this story in person. However, I didn't know any of this then. It took seven agonizing years before any of that happened. In 2004, I was neither here nor there, but it was time for me to take The Fool's journey.

Are you with me so far?

I • The Magician

The question is... Do you have everything you need to complete the mission? The Magician's answer is, "If you're hesitating to say yes, look *closer*, look *harder*, look *around* you." Did you notice that all four suit symbols in the traditional deck of Tarot are laid out on The Magician's table? So, if it *is* all laid out in front of you, why do you keep searching for more before making your move? Is it a lack of confidence? Is it stubbornness? Perhaps what you have to make this work wasn't all your ideas and resources, and perhaps it's arrogance that's keeping you from charging forward?

Whatever it is depends on you, or whoever is sitting in front of you, and the cards will help tell the story. It's up to you to *understand* the story, and more importantly, that whoever the reading is for *gets* the story.

Look at Jimi Hendrix. Jimi was a guitar player who was oozing talent from his pores, but he had one major obstacle growing up in the 1950s: He was left-handed. Most guitars back then were made for right-handed players. Rather than continue to look for a left-handed guitar, which was most likely beyond his means at the time, Jimi removed all of the guitar strings, turned the body of the instrument upside down, and restrung all six strings, which gave him a modified left-handed guitar. As Jimi attracted attention from record labels, there was pressure on him to sing lead vocals, as all superstars back then sang their own songs. If you listen to "Purple Haze," "Foxy Lady," and "Crosstown Traffic," you wouldn't confuse Jimi Hendrix with Pavarotti. He didn't have to be. The guitar was his attraction. How he played the guitar was what people wanted from him. His vocal style was very basic, almost spoken word, which didn't require a lot of crooning, but it fit the style of songs that allowed his virtuoso guitar playing to shine, while still allowing you to casually sing along with him.

My love for music started before I was old enough to walk or talk. My parents love to tell the story about Blondie's "Heart of Glass," which was my favorite song to dance to in my father's arms at just a year old. One day at a pizza place, it came on while I was in the stroller, and the radio cut out—which didn't sit well with a kid in what was probably a soiled diaper looking to rock out—and my tantrum was so loud that my parents took their cranky son home to play it on vinyl. So, growing up, it would seem obvious that becoming a musician would be in my future. I tried. I was awful. *I have the rhythm of a deaf turtle and the voice of a tortured cat who smokes way too many unfiltered cigarettes.* Yet, my love for music wouldn't subside. I needed to know *everything* about my favorite bands.

I would lie on the cold floor of my father's lanai every weekend and studied the liner notes of his albums. I listened to every single story those radio DJs told me. I wound up being able to hold conversations with people twice my age about music they grew up with. I was able to get them interested in the music I enjoyed while bridging gaps using stories and comparisons. I wrote my own songs with no way of ever getting them fleshed out. So, WTF was I doing with all of this knowledge? It didn't help me when I joined the electrical union and lasted all of two weeks before walking off the job. It didn't help me while bouncing in seedy Philly bars or delivering frozen food to school districts across Long Island. All I knew was music. Yet I couldn't play a single instrument worth a damn, and "Hot Cross Buns" on the recorder has been done a million times already. So, how could I apply all of this useless music knowledge and the ability to work it into any conversation?

One day, I heard a commercial for broadcasting school while making a food delivery. All of a sudden ... it made sense. Everything I knew, anything I could do well, suddenly had an outlet. I had a reason to tell you *why* Candlebox was unfairly treated by their Seattle contemporaries and *how* Bruce

Springsteen came up with the name for the E Street Band. Even the whole writing-my-own-songs thing manifested through my radio career, but we can get into that later. I learned that day that everything you need is already with you, if you are willing to get creative.

II • The High Priestess

There is a place where outward logic fails, and that inner voice roars. The High Priestess stands at that threshold.

How many times have you heard words come out of someone's mouth, and for some reason, you *know* that they mean something completely different than what we were all taught? Words that are simple and basic and should be taken at face value somehow seem to carry more than what's being shown to you. How many times have you simply 'had a feeling' without any evidence or even a single clue that would otherwise lead you to whatever profound conclusion you accurately assessed?

A song by Arrested Development that came on the radio often in the '90s always stood out to me. In "Mr. Wendal," they talk about the knowledge they received from a homeless person they encountered in their travels. At first glance, he's just your typical bum. I think it's fair to say that even the most compassionate of us would look at the person described in "Mr. Wendal" and, at best, buy them lunch or perhaps give them money for a few meals. I believe it's fair to say most of us wouldn't believe that Mr. Wendal, or anyone in his situation, would have anything to offer *us*.

However, the more you listen to the perspective of someone who doesn't have the stresses of a monthly mortgage or the pressure of maintaining an expected appearance, the easier it is to realize that simply understanding someone else's view is invaluable knowledge. You just wouldn't ever think so at first glance. To believe that a homeless person has anything that *you* would value takes patience, caring, and a softness not found in your everyday lifestyle.

When I was fourteen, I had a bit of a collision with the edge of a curb in the Birchfield housing complex in Mt. Laurel, NJ. It was during my two-week summer reprieve from Long Island, where things were far from stable. At my grandparents', I felt a sense of normalcy, and even if it was just temporary, I relished every moment, and each night I was out with my Jersey friends. I hoped it would last forever. Which was a big reason why the second my buddy Bruce tackled me into the sidewalk of West Peach Tree Court, I knew I was in trouble. It wasn't the pain that alarmed me. It was the *instant instinct* to go home. I just knew something was wrong.

On the surface, it was a bad scratch—the blood was minimal, and I heard worse sounds during Adam West's *Batman* TV show—but I knew something was wrong. My friends were even confused when I said goodbye and limped back to Grandma Jean and Pop Pop's, where my dad and grandfather were hanging out at the dining room table. Now, neither of these men was abusive, mean, or anything that's about to make them sound horrible, but when I asked them to take me to the hospital, I was met with indifference.

Then, after looking at my bruised but not mangled right knee, laughter set in. Then, a few less-than-masculine adjectives were sent my way. Then, like a college baseball player who was caught stealing despite his coach's hold sign, I was sent to the showers. As I feebly climbed the stairs, I would hear my grandmother question the decision to dismiss my concern, only to be assured by my grandfather that I was fine.

My time in South Jersey soon ended, and on the ride back to Long Island, something about my knee was bothering me. The scrapes had healed. The pain was gone. Yet something seemed off.

My mother's house just wasn't a fun place for me at fourteen. I was being raised by my mother and grandmother, and all I ever wanted was to be was away. So the moment I was dropped off, I was out at the baseball fields, just happy to be out. I never mentioned the incident in South Jersey because nothing was gonna slow me down.

I begged my way into a pickup softball game, and as soon as I swung at the first pitch, every one of my nagging suspicions reared its ugly head. My knee swelled up like a cantaloupe, and I was no longer able to put any pressure on it. Thankfully, there were pay phones at the park, and my mother was able to come and get me.

Once she got done yelling at me for interrupting *General Hospital*, she took a look at my knee. Then a longer look. Then she called in my grandmother. After a few minutes, they noticed an orange line making its way up my leg. The next thing I knew, I was in the emergency room with a staph infection and in immediate need of surgery.

Now, my mother was right. If I had gotten hurt at home, this would have never happened because every time I sneezed, we went to the doctor. However, in this situation, a little bit of that feminine, safer-than-sorry approach would have benefited me.

My parents divorced in 1981. This was 1992. I'll never forget the calmness in my mother's voice as she called my father from the hospital room phone:" John, it's your ex-wife. Remember when your son told you he hurt his knee and you ignored him? Well, he's in a hospital bed, about to get his leg cut open. I will see you in an hour." It was the only time I heard my mother speak to my father without yelling. It usually took an hour to get from Queens to Patchogue. He was in my hospital room within forty-five minutes.

Sometimes, it's that divine feminine side that leads you to the truth you seek.

III • The Empress

What is the difference between sexuality and sensuality?

Have you ever encountered someone who, on the surface, has everything you would find attractive? The curves, the hair, the look—yet somehow you're just not attracted? Sensuality isn't something easily faked. Either you have it, or you don't.

When I first heard Kim Carnes' version of "Bette Davis Eyes," I was in love. This wasn't during the time when you could just Google a picture, so the only image I had of Kim Carnes was the one her song created in my head. She was singing about a woman who would basically chew you up and spit you out, letting you come in so far just to destroy you, while somehow being compassionate about stomping on your heart. Why the hell was this appealing to me?

Have you heard the sound of Kim Carnes explaining this woman? Her sultry delivery was intoxicating. As intoxicating as the fresh air is to the avid hiker. As natural as the trees and the animals surrounding that hiker along his travels. It's more than just feminine. It's addictively feminine. It's unapologetically and naturally feminine.

My Grandma Grace always complained about how the girls my age dressed. "Who-uhs, Brian, they all dress like who-uhs. Why does everything have to be hanging out all of the time? We covered up in my day. No one needed to be out, exposed like a tramp." My grandmother passed away in 2019. She would have passed away again the second she saw Cardi B on the screen. Despite my grandmother's candidness, I always saw her take as unfair. In my eyes, these girls were just expressing their femininity.

I recently came across an old clip of Johnny Carson on YouTube featuring the singer Ann Margaret. I knew of her, but never got to see her perform. I swear my eyes never left that computer screen for the entire four minutes she sang. Every gyration, snarl, and gaze into the camera had me captivated. She could have been singing the phone book. I was hooked. No one moved like her. No one had that sexiness. Then I realized something. She was covered from head to toe. No cleavage, no midriff. And, as Grandma would say, "Nice to see her ass isn't hanging out." This was just femininity at its most pure.

IV • The Emperor

If I ask you to name an admirable leader, who comes to mind? Why? Forget about whether they are a famous person, politician, or hopefully someone you know on a personal level—what is it about them that led you to the word "leader"? Isn't there always one common thing overheard when talking about a great boss? "Man, my boss isn't afraid to roll up their sleeves and get dirty with us." When The Emperor comes up in a reading, this is the energy of someone you need to be open to in your life, or who you may be called to be.

Bruce Springsteen gave us the title track to his *Ghost of Tom Joad* album in 1995. The song borrows heavily from images expressed in the Woody Guthrie tune, "The Ballad of Tom Joad," which is inspired by the 1939 John Steinbeck novel, *The Grapes of Wrath*. Three sets of experiences, all writing about the same thing—sticking up for what's right, even if you're told it's wrong. There is a monologue during the bridge of Bruce's lead-off to the album that struck me. The narrator is letting his mother know that the easiest way to find him during his absence is to look for where injustice is taking place. Whether it's in the shape of a corrupt political system, the harshness of the economic landscape, or the wrong side of a righteous battle getting the upper hand, Bruce Springsteen's main character in "The Ghost of Tom Joad" promises to stand up for what's right, for who's right, and sees any time for these moments as being right.

Throughout a radio career that's spanned two decades, the fortune of getting to know some of the musicians who help define the sound of your station has presented itself more often than even I realized before doing some soul searching for this book.

Since 1993, one of my favorite obsessions has been the music of a band called Candlebox. Like Pearl Jam, Alice In Chains, Soundgarden, and Nirvana, i.e., the bands sat at the top of Grunge Mountain, Candlebox was also from Seattle, which seemed to be home to every single band that rose up in the '90s. But that didn't really matter to me. It was their lyrics. They reached an angry fifteen-year-old kid deeper than any other band. Than any other person. I heard Kevin Martin's lyrics louder than my teacher's lessons. Clearer than my parents ' warnings. Crisper than my therapist's message.

As my career progressed and I was fully established as a morning show host on a rock radio station, my relationship with Kevin Martin grew from a simple, convenient work relationship to friendship, and as of today, a full-blown brotherhood. He's taught me more about dealing with the public wanting from you than any book could illustrate. He's been an ear to listen and never speaks until he's heard all you have to say. I can gush all day with stories, but there was one moment he shared with me that will help explain who The Emperor represents better than all of them.

It was May 18, 2017. The news of Chris Cornell's suicide ripped through the rock music world like a violent storm. I spent my thirty-minute ride to the radio station numb. I couldn't form a single coherent thought about how I was going to break this news. Nothing made sense. This wasn't just one of my favorite singers, this was a voice that helped define who my generation was and carried memories of how we all came to be. This was the lead singer of Soundgarden. Of Audioslave. Of Temple of the Dog. A voice we play and listen to on 94.3 The Shark at least five times a day.

At 5:55 a.m., right before my first break, I honestly thought to myself, *How would Kevin handle this?* At 6:05 a.m., I said hello, apologized for the shakiness in my voice, and delivered the news with honesty, compassion, and a realization that it was my job to do so. By 9 a.m., the amount of phone calls and shared tears was as motivating as they were cathartic, and our little rock community was getting through it—together.

Then, at 9:27 a.m., I got a text. I'll never forget it. It was Kevin asking me if I was okay and telling me that he was around if I needed to talk.

Now ... I am a rock music nerd. I live, breathe, and sleep grunge music. Chris Cornell's passing was a knife through my bitter Gen-X heart. But I didn't know Chris Cornell. I never got the chance to meet him. It was not even 6:30 a.m. in California when Kevin Martin heard the news about his friend, someone who he has referred to as a beautiful human being many times in interviews with me, and yet he took time to check on his buddy on the other side of the world, offering help despite his pain, despite his mourning.

That ... *that* is The Emperor.

V • The Hierophant

How many times have you heard the expression *slow and steady wins the race*? You probably heard it when you dropped the tray of soda on the floor trying to keep up with the happy hour rush, or when a loved one said it to you after you showed them your speeding ticket. Most likely, you thought about punching anyone who said it to you. But did you ever think about why that expression is still around?

It's basic. It's proven. It's safe. It's never been said by anyone who hasn't felt the repercussions of racing through the process.

The Hierophant represents proven values, or at least what are widely believed to be proven values. If you're seeking guidance for your injured back, you wouldn't consult some online quack who will rub his combo of sea salt and peanut butter on your problem area for $19.95, plus shipping. If you're being called to teach, it's from the textbooks that you learned from, not the cutting-edge experimental style, where there are no wrong answers and everyone gets an "A" and a hug.

George Harrison spent more time in India than the rest of The Beatles. His passion for Hindu culture and Eastern Indian music was evident throughout some of the Fab Four's most well-known songs. The sitar he plays on The Beatles' "Norwegian Wood" is a traditional Hindustani string instrument that dates back to the eighteenth century. The Beatles were a *rock* band. It took a lot of testicular fortitude to introduce such a thing to rock audiences, but it worked. George didn't play the sitar like a guitar. He didn't make it sound like a rock instrument. He brought an ancient sound to modern music *as is*, which turned a lot of hippie kids on to musicians like Ravi Shankar, and influenced other bands such as The Rolling Stones and Metallica to incorporate Eastern instruments into their music. The introduction was done by simply sticking to the traditional sound and style of the instrument and trusting that it was enough, as is, to reach a new audience.

Listen to any demo of any radio DJ's first shift. It's horrible. No, not just raw or unpolished. It's *awful*. The anticipation of doing my first radio shift on a rock radio station was all-consuming; all I could think about was getting to the station. It was an hour ride to WJSE in Linwood, NJ, and the entire sixty minutes was spent singing along to *The Greatest American Hero* theme song, but with one minor change: I kept paraphrasing the chorus with "Believe it or not, I'm *talking* on air!"

Yeah, if you threw this book away and stopped talking to me, I would understand. If you're still here, I hope I painted the picture of how special this moment was to me.

I walked into that studio with a note from my boss, Scotty, that I still have today. "Brian," it begins, "have fun today. Don't try to do too much. Just front and back sell the songs and move on, and remember to just talk," which meant to simply talk about what was played, and then what I was about to play, and then turn the mic off. Now, it wasn't that I thought Scotty's advice was bad or that I was better than that. It's just that the second that "on-air" light went on, my mind went into *overdrive*. I wanted my new listeners to know *all* of the geeky music facts I knew. And listening back, I must have thought all of South Jersey was deaf, because I screamed louder than a professional wrestler on live TV in pursuit of the heavyweight championship.

The moment got to me, and I tried to do too much. Keeping it simple would have kept me on the air longer, but unfortunately, I couldn't grasp the concept. After a few months, I got another shot. This time, I waited a while before adding more elements of my knowledge and personality to my delivery. I listened to what my experienced mentors in the business shared with me. They were right. Once the basics were mastered, I got to have a *lot* of fun in this business.

VI • The Lovers

The one phrase I repeat to my students above all others is one that often takes them a minute to process. "When you read someone, you're seeing them fully naked." Now, as often as you may say to yourself, "I will only see what the person coming to me will allow me to see," you are going to see things in people all of the time that you weren't expecting. That is mostly because they aren't expecting to be so open, and they weren't planning to be so honest.

In most decks, both representatives of The Lovers are letting it all hang out for you to see. It's common for this card to be taken at first glance as a harmonious and blissful true love. But like everything we learn past a fifth-grade reading level, The Lovers is just a little bit more complex than the relationships we learned about in nursery rhymes. Sometimes, the best relationships don't give us everything we need, and sometimes, just because we have everything we need doesn't mean we're in the best relationships.

Since we just spoke of Kevin Martin of Candlebox while looking at The Emperor, let's take a look at an often overlooked project he was a part of in the early 2000s called the HiWatts. On their one album, *The Possibility of Being*, the song "The Lovers" talks about a relationship that is seemingly in the past. The couple in the song shared a love that was pure and raw, but while leaving themselves wide open to each other, it left them vulnerable to a world that didn't have time for their exploration of each other. As the song progresses, we find out that too much was sacrificed for this love to last. Yet it was important enough to still reflect upon, and even to celebrate. We will always have choices. What's best for you, what's best for "us," and many of life's choices are decided as we learn to balance them. The Lovers is a call to start figuring that out.

The most vulnerable I ever felt was in the middle of March of 2019, as I watched my marriage—my second marriage—dissolve before my eyes. Here I was, a two-time loser in the game of life, leaving yet another union before two years had passed me by. The amount of frustration and embarrassment that pinned me down was outweighed only by my desire to bury my feelings.

Within a month, I found myself entranced by a mysterious brunette whose attractiveness was baffling to me. Yes, she was attractive. Yes, she was flirtatious. But still, the fact was I was stupid enough to get involved with someone before the ink on my divorce papers dried. If I told you the additional circumstances surrounding how stupid it was to open myself up to this woman, you would slap me. But none of that really matters now. I was drawn to this woman on a level that I couldn't figure out, and that not only pissed me off but drew me closer to her.

One day, she confessed a guilty feeling that she had carried with her for years about her ex-husband, who had passed away. Now, to listen to the story, you would absolutely understand why she left before he eventually self-destructed, but you would also feel every moment of her pain for simply being human and wondering what would have happened had she stayed. As her tears stained my console while we watched the waves wash up on the sand through my windshield, my attraction to her became crystal clear.

When I was eighteen, I chose to hang out with some friends I hadn't seen in a while because some girls were going to be there. My best friend, who I blew off that night for the chance to get laid, drove past my house on his motorcycle, didn't see my car, and kept going. A few blocks later would be the last time he rode on that bike, and all I can think of these years later is that he left us doing what he loved. As this girl shared her pain, I realized immediately why she never left my head. She understood *my* pain. She saw the invisible boulder I carried at all times and never flinched because she too knew what it was like to drag such an emotional attachment around with her.

I don't think she and I lasted another month due to many circumstances that, like I said, were clearly obvious to everyone else but us. But yet, this short time we spent together still proves extremely valuable to me. Because of that tryst, I realized that I would only open myself up that honestly again to someone who could handle it. And it was with someone who could handle it that I would make a lasting relationship in my life.

VII • The Chariot

Can you think of an incident that made you stronger? That made you say, "I will never let anything slow me down again"? Before that very moment, how many times had you said to yourself, "I would have finished writing this book if I didn't let my parents or my spouse fill my head with doubt," or "I'd be skinny right now if my husband stopped taking us out for fatty meals," or "I'd be able to workout if my kids didn't demand so much of my time." How about this one? "I'd be able to go back to school and learn how to do what I really want to do if everyone stopped demanding so much from me."

The Chariot is that *enough* card. Here are my boundaries and here are my fucking requirements—and I'm not asking you for them, I'm *telling* you what they are! It's a card that often gets associated with travel, but travel is a metaphor. It can mean a relocation or a move, if that's what you are unapologetically searching for.

Kiss is a band that was unapologetic in their desire to make money through music. The commercial moves they made as they built their empire would have fans crying *sellout* if it were any other group of musicians. They wore face paint as a gimmick and took it off as a publicity stunt. They made a *disco* song. They put the makeup back on. I saw their last tour at Jones Beach in August of 2000. I was twenty-two. In 2024, when I was forty-five, they announced their "last" two shows at Madison Square Garden. They were never shy about their goal: complete and total monetization of their music empire. Rock and roll integrity be damned. Gene Simmons wrote a song called "It's My Life," which would be the battle cry for The Chariot. Kiss never officially recorded it in the studio, but The Demon under the face paint did give the song to the Plasmatics. Wendy O. Williams sings of relishing in the disdain for her rule-breaking reputation and boasting about her choices being solely her own, and for her only. If The Chariot card in your deck could speak, you would hear the lyrics to "It's My Life."

Growing up as the first-born Italian male, expectations were set for me before I knew what my favorite binky was. The problem was, those expectations bored the heck out of me. My father worked hard as a mechanic. Extremely hard, and I admired him for it. But that never meant I wanted to *live* that life. Seventeen-hour days, six days a week, he was under a car. He worked a full-time job fixing cars for a shop and then came home and worked his side business, fixing cars in his own garage. I can still hear the disappointment in my grandfather's voice when I was a teenager. "I don't understand, Brian. Why don't you want to learn how to fix cars like your father? You don't think he has enough?"

To this day, I don't think my family verbally said to themselves that I couldn't be more successful or happier than my father, but their attitude has always been to work for one person as long as you can, save all your money, and hope you have enough before you die one day. Any sort of career that threatened that glorious lifestyle was immediately dismissed as stupid. "Unrealistic" was a word I heard often growing up.

When I finally decided that driving a truck for a living wasn't fulfilling my needs and robbed Peter to pay Paul for broadcasting school, I wasn't expecting a warm showing of encouragement. That was pretty much the final straw of my deteriorating relationship with Pop Pop. One day, he fell ill and wound up in the hospital. I took the day off from my day job to drive my grandmother and my uncle up to see him. After an hour, I explained that I needed to leave so I could make it to class that night. To this day, I remember his tirade. He told me that he didn't want to hurt me with what he was about to say, but for my own good I needed to know how selfish I was for pursuing a radio career, how stupid it was that I didn't listen to his advice and my father's advice, and how what I'm doing is hurting everyone, but I was too self-absorbed to see it. His final sentence was the punch line: "You have a better chance of being struck by lightning than getting into radio."

A few weeks later, I had my first shift at 102.7 The Ace, Atlantic City's rock station. God, I sucked. But that's not important. What was important was that I was doing life my way—until lightning hit the building and knocked me off the air. I could have cried. But I didn't. I remembered how hard I worked to get into that studio. I waited the storm out, and just before my shift was over, the power came back on. I jumped on my Chariot and finished my shift.

VIII • Strength

Can you think of a situation that's tested your convictions? Can you think of one that would?

I used to scoff at those religious memes about God putting you through so much pain because he knew you could withstand it. I still find them rage-inducing, depending on how much commuter traffic I dealt with that day. But if you slightly reword it, it not only doesn't sound so full of shit, but it makes a lot of sense, too. If you were never challenged to be strong, how would you ever know how strong you really are?

There is a song I always play when it comes time to negotiate. Whether it's a new contract, a business situation, or when it's time to finally open my mouth to a friend, loved one, or acquaintance who's gotten too comfortable with how they've spoken to me, I listen to "Waking Lions" by the Michigan-based band Pop Evil. The lyrics start out with the narrator questioning if there is a better option than plunging into the battle he's expecting, but still being very clear about how there is no apprehension to do so. Whatever was done to him, this is the last time it's going to happen. He talks of standing as tall as a skyscraper and warns that the animal has been woken inside of him. All that he endured has led him to this moment. Instead of allowing himself to be beaten down, he realizes that his scars have healed, and all that's left are the lessons learned from them. He can't be hurt anymore.

Most bands that I have worked with through my career have been awesome to talk to. Management, not so much. And it's easy to understand why. Some reasons are completely justifiable; some are just self-serving bullshit designed solely to justify some of these people having jobs. That's how I see it, and I doubt you're gonna change my mind.

Many times, Rob, my radio partner, and I would drive to a music venue for a scheduled band interview only to be blown off at the last second, despite weeks of promoting and helping out behind the scenes to make the show a success. One of the other agreements for these types of situations is that the DJs are granted about 120 seconds before a show to greet the audience, rile them up, and do what's called a "soft intro," which usually takes place about five minutes before the band takes the stage. In only a few dozen occasions, we waited for hours for a tour manager to get us set up, only to get a text like, "Where are you guys?" five minutes *after* the first song is playing. Let me add that we don't get paid for these. We do them because it's important to be in front of our listeners in a setting outside of the car radio. We do it because, after helping to promote a show for weeks and sometimes months in advance, it's a small ask, despite any inconvenience our two minutes may have.

One Halloween night, a very prominent band from the '90s was playing The Paramount in Huntington. I was already jaded from being blown off for interviews and stage announcements from two other bands that month, and I wasn't really confident that this wasn't a waste of time. The band members themselves were great and made it into the studio for a meet and greet with some lucky listeners. We then got an email from the tour manager saying that we needed to be backstage at 8:35 p.m. because the band was going on at 8:50 p.m., and their rule was ten minutes before the show. That was stated in black and white. The opening band's time was then extended, so this particular headliner would be taking the stage at 9:30 p.m. Rob and I arrived at 9:15 p.m., only to be told we blew it because we were supposed to meet them forty-five minutes ago. They weren't nice. I showed this guy his own words, and he told me it wasn't his problem.

Now, of the two of us, I'm the hothead. So maybe this was inevitable, but an entire fiasco started to unfold. The Paramount manager was completely on our side and trying to reason with this guy who was acting like he found out his wife had cheated on him just seconds ago. Nothing was getting through to this guy. Suddenly, He-Man walks up to us. I'm not kidding. It was Halloween night, and their bodyguard was dressed like He-Man. "What's the fucking problem?" he bellowed. Things didn't seem to be going well in Enternia either, and we were getting the brunt of it all. Rob and The Paramount manager pleaded their case that we were promised stage announcements and that we followed every rule thrown at us, but they kept getting the same response: "Not our problem."

Now, radio is a very small community. For as many jocks as there may be in the U.S. alone, we all know each other or know someone that knows everyone else. This ran through my head as I stood there fuming, and all words faded into white noise. I thought of the repercussions of what my imminent explosion might bring to the station as I tried my best to rationalize in my head the best response to all of this. Then I began hearing the outside conversation again. Rob was gently explaining how much of this band's music we play on our station and the reply was, "I don't give a fuck." Now, I only remember what I said because it's still talked about to this day—and you can be the judge on whether that's a good thing or a bad thing.

"Oh yeah, asshole?" I said. "How about we pull your fucking band's songs, huh? How about you go tell them the next time there's thirty fucking people in the crowd that it was your fucking fault because you wouldn't give us two fucking minutes to greet our listeners? These guys haven't had a fucking hit since 1994, but we keep playing them, so let's see what happens next time you're in fucking town."

Keep in mind, at this point, I was yelling at some troll-looking dude who was standing next to He-Man, who, by the way, suddenly lost his tan. I don't remember exactly what was said because it was the mid-2010s, but we got our stage announcements. Now, let me just say that I was completely in the wrong about their last hit being in 1994. It was 2005.

When The Strength card shows up, you have accepted and see your worth, and you have what it takes to deal with anyone who doesn't.

IX • The Hermit

Can you think of a reason for a reclusive break that isn't because everything in your life is a disaster? What can possibly happen in life that would encourage you to step back from the crowd for a little while and catch your breath?

Imagine spending all of your energy and most of your bank account on a Cancun getaway with some friends. After a week of clubbing, drinking on the beach, and God knows what you did with who, you would probably need a few days alone in your room. Heck, all you could probably afford after an excursion like that would be memories. How about after your wedding? The planning is over. The disgruntled family members who couldn't bring their third cousin and their pet goldfish got over it. And the band got your first dance right. You're exhausted. This would be a good time to lie in bed with your spouse and count your cards. Maybe you have an exam that could lead to a life-changing upgrade *if* you pass, and you can't afford any distractions.

We started with these because it's easy to think of all the negative reasons to need a break. A death in the family. A bad breakup. Mental illness. Overwhelming news that takes time to digest, and so on.

After *The River* tour in 1980, in which Bruce Springsteen and the E Street Band toured the world while rocking packed arenas, and it was becoming clear that the future was only getting brighter, the Boss made the decision to turn inward. His songwriting in Colts Neck, NJ, by himself in his kitchen, was all we got from that time he chose to step back. The imagery in these songs is dark—spree killings, cop killings, having no hope for a better life except winning the lottery. The collection of songs we got from Bruce Springsteen on September 30, 1982, wasn't the triumphant return of rock and roll's phenom, but instead the reflection of a man who stepped aside for a moment to see what the mirror had to say. He didn't tour the *Nebraska* album. Instead, he chose to play New Jersey bars for most of the year. By the time his vacation from the rock and roll spotlight had ended, the world rejoiced in welcoming New Jersey's favorite son back into their lives. *Born in the U.S.A.* catapulted the band into the stratosphere, dwarfing any success they previously enjoyed. And thanks to the energy of The Hermit, Bruce was ready.

I experienced my first divorce back in 2014. I was doing morning radio in Westchester, about one hour from where I recently lived, and desperately needed a new place to live. The obvious move was to find somewhere close to work and start a new life—a life away from what I left behind—and embrace what had become my new world. Except for one problem: I wasn't ready. I wasn't ready for anything new.

I needed a place to live, yeah. But this idea of a new landlord, new neighbors, a new place to get sandwiches, made me sick. Seriously. I went from a wife and a young stepson and a deli that made the best coleslaw to limbo—and I wasn't ready to leave yet. So I did what any rational thirty-five-year-old would do. I went back to Grandma's house and slept on the couch for a few months. Now, I knew I couldn't stay there forever. There were only so many times a guy could be woken up in the middle of the night to ensure he was still breathing before he went insane. But for a short while, it was just fine. It was fine because I knew the crazy I was living in. It was my childhood crazy. My familiar crazy. I wasn't ready for new yet, and during the time I felt this, Grandma Grace enjoyed having her Hermit back.

X • Wheel of Fortune

What do you think it looks like to others as you actively pursue your goals? How would this burning desire to conquer any obstacle on your path look to others who may not necessarily know you? Would *you* understand being treated that way?

I've heard the Wheel of Fortune be referred to as the "karmic card," and I'm not going to be the one to argue that logical interpretation. I always think of the lyrics to Lynyrd Skynyrd's "Simple Man" when the Wheel of Fortune comes up. As the wise mother sits her son down for a talk, you realize quickly that these are hopes she has for her beloved child, but not expectations. You get the sense she realizes he's to make his own path, but she hopes that, while doing so, he keeps this conversation in mind. The advice is easy enough to understand. Be patient and modest. Keep your beliefs in yourself and your faith, whatever that may be. Be a good person. And if you follow all of this, her fears of you making it out in the harsh world will be extremely minimal. Mama believes fully that if her son is a good person, good things will happen, and he will continue along that cycle throughout his life.

One of my first experiences at a successful rock station was as a promotions intern for 95.9 The WRAT in Belmar, NJ. My family didn't understand why I would drive an hour to work for free, and they didn't understand the value I saw in gaining experience at a successful radio station that played the music I loved. They also didn't know about the number of women I'd encounter who were grateful to accept the T-shirts, concert tickets, and gift cards I was handing out at every hopping bar along the Jersey Shore. So, I didn't mind working for free, but I *was* looking for the type of hands-on education you couldn't get from a teacher sitting in a classroom desk chair.

All of the jocks were cool. As long as you didn't hang off the side of them, they would talk to you. And if you were quick enough to pick up what they were laying down, you would learn. However, that didn't mean their boundary wasn't rightfully visible to a near-sighted bat. The promo team would lug the speakers, the rack system, the massive inflatable rat, and bins and bins of prizes in extreme heat, and the jocks would be oblivious to our struggle. Except for one.

Jimmy Steel was insistent on grabbing one handle on a four-foot speaker cabinet and walking with you side-by-side through the crowded bar to set up. I can't remember how many times he objected to my request that he relax before the gig because he was the talent. If we were working, Jimmy was working. That always stuck with me.

A few years later, *I* was the talent, and when I grabbed one side of the big retractable tent at a festival, my promo kid looked at me like I just presented him with a calculus equation NASA couldn't figure out. Looking at his confused expression, I asked him what was wrong. I'll never forget his response:" Nothing," he said. "I've been here five years, and none of the jocks ever helped us before." My smile must have lit up that entire field we were standing in.

"Just remember this when you're the jock, kiddo," I replied.

XI • Justice

Have you ever done the right thing despite knowing there would be fallout from others who couldn't see your perspective? Have you ever stood your ground despite being the only one in the room who felt this way? Remember this phrase: *Doing what's right is almost never doing what's easy.*

Now, quick, what comes to mind the second you hear the phrase "Fair is fair"? If you picture Helen Slater pumping both fists over her blonde crew cut while staring defiantly into the news camera, you have definitely hurt your lower back sneezing. You also saw a great 1980s flick in *The Legend of Billie Jean.* The heroine in that story became one simply by standing up for what she knew was right. In the plot, Helen Slater's character gets her family into trouble as a result of looking to repair her brother's vandalized scooter. Despite now being on the run, due to a self-defense shooting as she was being assaulted by the bike shop owner, she maintains that she's willing to face the consequences as long as her brother is reimbursed for his scooter, rejecting any other reward that is now coming with her growing fame as an antihero. Whatever resulted from her actions for doing what was right, she was willing to face it, as long as the reason she was fighting was met with the justice she felt it deserved.

Pat Benatar's theme song for the movie, titled "Invincible," talks about feeling the power in your conviction. Her lyrics warn that there isn't time to wonder about your innocence when what you're facing doesn't really care what you think. You're in a battle. You think you're right, and there is no longer any time to second-guess that. What's done is done, and now we're gonna find out what happens next. In the do-or-die moments of battle, those who truly believe they are on the right side of the fight will always feel invincible. Justice is asking you if you're standing strong enough in that belief as it all plays out.

Another term for a DJ is "radio personality." In the world of broadcasting, personality isn't just a noun; it's a wrecking ball of a verb, which crashes through every single company just looking to keep the ratings high enough to sell commercial spots. In twenty years, I've seen more than enough companies get "personality-ed" by DJs and programmers who have embraced the belief of being bigger than the radio station.

The painfully vanilla midday host, who is usually also the program director (which is just a fancy way of saying "boss"), gives themselves all of the paid appearances and the best ticket giveaways, despite being better served in other day parts. They're incessant martyrs who cry daily about being overworked, but suddenly develop a hearing problem when you offer to take some responsibilities off their hands. They're people who do what's best for them and ignore the bigger picture.

After a few years, and my third program director (PD) within that time, being the morning-show host on a local rock radio station stopped being fun. I soon lost my patience as the new PD began changing all of my production work, taking away my writing and promotions responsibilities, and diminishing the importance of the morning drive position, all the while crying louder and louder to me about how busy he was.

My dignity took a hit, too, as I realized how long I listened to this asshole complain to me how he had no help, while mysteriously failing to comprehend my multiple offers to do just that. I made a point to the operations manager that a radio contest where the listener had to listen to the 11 a.m. to 1 p.m. midday girl for the password to win tickets from the 2 p.m. to 7 p.m. afternoon drive guy—who in this case was also the PD—made no sense. It's just not done this way, and I explained that I once again felt like I was being excluded from my own radio station. The operations manager shrugged it off. "He's the PD," he said. "He can give the tickets away however he wants."

Okay, I thought, fuck this. I'm done. I can't win if they take away my sword and send me into battle with my hands tied behind my back, and I wasn't getting paid enough to endure that kind of ass kicking. In a rare moment during my pre-belief era, I asked my mother to throw some cards on a Saturday as I got ready to resign the following Monday. She said they weren't gonna let me go, and if I quit, I'd be back in fifteen minutes.

I walked in that Monday and quit. The OM tried to reason with me to stay by showing me everything from his perspective, all the while diminishing my feelings on everything that was wrong. It was predictable, aggravating, and satisfying, as I had no doubt that I was making the right move. I left the building smiling.

As I started my car, the clock said 11:01 a.m. At 11:16 a.m., my general manager called. I refused to pick it up. I wasn't in the mood to talk, and I was in less of a mood to admit that my mother and her voodoo witchy crap was pinpoint accurate, down the second.

Now, my job is far from perfect. But it's much better than before. As of this writing, I've celebrated my tenth year as a morning-show host. The package I was offered since my line was drawn is a much more livable and reasonable one. I didn't get the higher title I demanded. I received very little representation during future battles, which was promised. I knew there would be compromises once the verdict was rendered. My compensation was increased dramatically. My creative freedom was reasonably restored. Listenership on the radio station I anchored on the morning drive returned, and suddenly it seemed important again. I felt I was right. I was no longer willing to accept any other opinion on it. Justice was served, and I was more than willing to accept the outcome.

XII • The Hanged Man

A furniture salesman once told me the most popular saying in his business was, "There is an ass for every chair." In Tarot, there is a situation for every card. We just talked about the fight energy of the Justice card and the conviction behind the decision to battle. The Hanged Man represents a completely different scenario that you've been in.

What are some situations that you knew were impossible to win? Can you think back to a time when it was better to give up than to continue to fight?

I always think back to the Cheap Trick song "Surrender" when The Hanged Man shows up in a reading. It's the idea of giving up without completely giving in, just as lead singer Robin Zander pleads with us during the song's chorus. The narrator of the song is irritated that his authoritarian parents have laid down some extremely rigid parameters for his existence. His frustration only grows at the realization that they themselves do not live by the same rules they force him to follow. You know, typical teenage angst stuff. But yet, you do feel that because of this realization, he can probably get away with a lot more if he simply goes about his business and flies under the radar. If he doesn't fight his parents, they'll be too busy being hypocrites to notice.

During my first brief marriage, I became a stepfather. It was as rewarding as it was challenging. I regret nothing about that time, and I truly believe I'm a more understanding person for having been involved in the upbringing of a four-year-old. The problem was that my ex-wife and I just couldn't make it work. The hows and whys don't matter anymore. At the time, we both thought we were one hundred percent right. We shared an apartment, and despite feeling that I was the one being wronged, we had a major decision to make. The landlords had expressed their hope that I would be the one who stayed. My ex-wife, however, wasn't having it.

I didn't really have a place to go. In theory, the apartment was mine, and I had the advantage in a battle to keep it. In reality, it wasn't going to serve anyone if we all lost, which was seemingly inevitable. My ex-wife had a small child. Despite the ugliness of a divorce, I still cared deeply for them both, at least enough to realize this wasn't a battle worth fighting. I crashed on couches for a few weeks before settling back in with my grandmother, as I mentioned earlier. It was a minor respite while I got my bearings.

I felt like a hanged man, swinging in the wind. But I also felt every wound that was administered during my last war, and I wasn't ready to fight again just yet. So, I dealt with the inconvenience of being effectively homeless and accepted help from my family, despite being in my thirties. Within a few months, it all worked out. But for the time being, I was The Hanged Man.

XIII • Death

Think back to a situation that changed your life forever—changed it in a way where the day it happened was the last day you were ever fully that person. Situations like this are usually sudden and abrupt, but not always. When it ends, though, there is no doubt that you will never be the same again.

Growing up in the '90s meant you spent a lot of time arguing over stupid things that today you can solve with a frantic thumbing of a Google search. The only thing more obnoxious than a drunken argument over sports was a drunken argument over music. Decades have passed, and even with the advent of the internet, grown metalheads still argue over the fate of Ozzy's woman in the Black Sabbath song "Changes." The only thing more melancholy than the emotional pounding of the song's piano notes is the haunting tone of loss in the legendary frontman's voice. The way Ozzy sings of her loss still has many thinking that she passed away. But if you listen closely beyond the narrator's sadness, you learn that it was he who said goodbye, as he admits early on that he let her go. It's easy to get lost in the magnitude of his loss to miss that line, just as you can get lost in the haunting depiction of the Death card in most Tarot decks.

No card can make a person grab a paper bag and frantically hyperventilate into it faster than the Death card. The irony is that it almost never means death, but the death *of something* that was a huge part of you. Ozzy sure sounds like he's dying in that song, as he relates the pain of screwing up the one woman he loved more than anything. No matter what, he wasn't going to be the same. Some breakups can be like that. You're so used to life being one way that when it finally happens, it feels sudden, no matter how long the writing had been on the wall. It's the same with losing a toxic job that you held most of your life.

Remember at the beginning of this book when we took The Fool's journey, and I had left everything to start over in the South? A few months before that, I had met a friend out in Mt. Laurel, where I had been visiting my grandparents. I'd spent every summer there since I was five, so I knew some people in town and wanted to get a drink. There was only so much reunion-ing I could do in one trip without a vodka back then. For some stupid reason, I could feel the presence of a girl behind me feeding the jukebox her hard-earned money.

Some in this situation would say hello or offer a drink. I can still remember my line to this day: "Yo, honey! We're in South Jersey. How come there's no Bruce Springsteen on this jukebox?" Turns out Bruce was her favorite too, and not just the "Yeah, I have *Born in the U.S.A.* somewhere in my attic" type of fan. She spoke the language. Her favorite song, "Bobby Jean," is the same one I have the lyrics to tattooed on my forearm.

When I left Long Island and everything I knew for a new unknown, it was supposed to be with her. I had metaphorically burned the George Washington Bridge behind me as I crossed over it. I arrived with nothing. Soon after, I had even less because she got cold feet and moved in with her best friend instead. With nowhere to go, I scrambled to find a hole-in-the-wall apartment I couldn't afford on my own and struggled horribly. She eventually moved in, but the damage was done, and my trust in her was irreparable. Desperately, we tried to make it work, and it probably would have, but I was too stubborn and hurt by being abandoned. Yet we stuck it out for *seven years*. During that time, we fought a lot. Useless, needless fights. We grew more and more miserable, yet somehow we managed to find plenty of bright spots—bright spots that could have stayed lit, if only I could come to trust her. But I never could.

Meanwhile, I gave up truck driving and bartended my way through broadcasting school. When I finally landed a job back home, she talked about coming back with me. She even interviewed for a few jobs in Long Island before reality set in, and it all melted down. We were done. I was leaving, she was staying, and no matter what we had done during those seven years, nothing was gonna change that.

Two days before I left, the universe let me know just how finished our relationship was. On June 18, 2011, as Bruce Springsteen sings in "Tenth Avenue Freeze-Out," "They made that change uptown." Clarence Clemons, Bruce Springsteen's beloved saxophone player, left us. The "Big Man," so to speak, "joined the band." To lose a seven-year relationship that started with a common love for all things Springsteen was rough; to lose the most popular member of that band on top of it was almost comical. Almost. In reality, it was crushing.

The next day, my now ex and I listened to a tribute to Clarence on the radio while I packed my things. They played all the songs we used to sing together. As I walked out the door, the reality hit me that Clarence, my musical hero, was never coming back—and neither was I. Things were never gonna be the same. I drove home that night numb. But when I crossed the bridge back home, a smile crept onto my face. I was coming home. This was a new beginning.

The next day, I did my first shift at my new station in my hometown. When I saw my first song, I started bawling. "What's up, Long Island!" I began. "I'm Orlando." The first song we got to listen to together was Bruce's "Rosalita."

No matter how you look at the Death card, the change it predicts might be hard. But your happiness is never over. If you're reading this book, you'll probably agree that, even if the death was literal, it's never over. It won't be what you once knew, but that's the point.

XIV • Temperance

You know how certain people can set your emotions off kilter? Perhaps being in certain places can offset your balance. Temperance isn't about getting everything even. It's about getting everything *balanced*. When we realize we're moving too far into one direction, what's one instinct we all seem to have at some point in our lives? We immediately turn around, blow right past the middle, and try to get too far in the opposite direction in some righteous quest to even it all out. That gets exhausting. That's when Temperance can show up to remind you why you're suddenly so emotionally drained.

Depeche Mode wrote a song that would be the entrance music for Temperance if it were a professional wrestler or talk show host. It was their seventh single, 1983's "Get the Balance Right." The band was one of the driving forces of the early '80s "new wave" music movement and fearlessly put out an album of this new type of music every year for the first four years of its existence. Four albums in just over twelve hundred days is mind-blowing. Some bands can't make a second record in four years, but here was Depeche Mode, carrying the new wave music flag into a new decade with ferocity. While still one of the more prolific bands to come into our lives, they never again put out more than two albums in consecutive years, having at least one year between albums after 1987. Perhaps they were *getting the balance right*.

Since I was a young kid, I struggled with my weight. Although there are much gentler ways to describe a young me in today's society, I was your typical fat kid. Sad, bullied, awkward. If you look through photos of me throughout my four-and-a-half decades on the planet, searching only for my physical shape to document, you'd get whiplash. Starting as a young teen and well into my adult life, I'd get bursts of inspiration where I would swear off bread for months and live at the gym for stretches so long that people would forget I still lived in the neighborhood. Then I'd show up with my hard-earned new physique, embrace the attention, and, in a matter of months, proceed to piss away all of my effort and be out of shape again.

Rinse and repeat. Over and over again. I can't remember a time when I just breathed easy about my weight and said, "This is good. I can just live within ten pounds of this between winter and summer and be happy." If I wasn't racing to get the weight off, I was rushing to put it back on. Temperance would tell me to stop swinging from one extreme to the other and simply get back to the middle—and breathe.

XV • The Devil

Nobody is ready for The Devil when he shows up. The longer we tend to avoid reality, the harder it hits us in the face when it inevitably catches up.

No addict starts off by telling you they're an addict. Nobody in an abusive relationship advertises it. Most cutters wear long sleeves. Everything is always okay. It's okay, and you're just being irrational. To combat the guilt that weighs on someone lying to the world, they submerge it into whatever river of lies and deceit they are living in. When they're just about out of oxygen, they'll come up for air, far from prepared to handle any concern you may have. So back down under they go.

The Devil is here to remind us that there is nowhere left to hide. You're out of breath, and if you keep your head in the water any longer to avoid the facts, you're going to drown. Layne Staley sings of this dance with the Devil in many of Alice In Chains 'standout tracks, but in the 1992 song "Godsmack," the Devil is quite prominent. The narrator seems to be battling his own conscience, if not the Devil himself, as he realizes his fragile excuse of doing drugs "just for fun" is no fun at all. Layne Staley eventually lost his battle with his demons in 2002, leaving behind a modest body of work with an extraordinary tale of caution attached. Whatever your unhealthy attachments are, when the Devil shows up, it's not that no one else believes your denial anymore—it's that you have lost the ability to con yourself.

During our discussion about the previous card, we talked about my ongoing battle with weight loss. For most of my life, it was the rate of the methods I used to get skinny that I abused more than the methods themselves being abusive.

When I first transitioned into full-time morning radio back in 2011 after years of doing nights and afternoons, a whole new set of obstacles presented themselves, as I was now on a schedule the Devil himself wouldn't sentence his worst tenants to. I had gone from the convenience of an empty gym during an 11 a.m. workout before my 2 p.m. afternoon drive shift, with plenty of room for messing around, to being up early enough to wake the roosters and having no time to do anything at the same speed as anyone else. To this day, by 2 p.m., most morning show hosts will tell you that it feels like you're moving through quicksand. I remember waking up one morning to the clock reading 4 a.m. and frantically running for the door while simultaneously putting on yesterday's clothes, only to be greeted by the blazing sun and realizing it was actually 4 p.m.

To combat this jarring change, I started guzzling disgusting amounts of pre-workout formulas and energy drinks to make it through a shift. Then I'd shove lunch down my throat because I needed to eat before the gym. But at that point, I was sluggish from eating too much, so I'd have another energy drink to get through a workout and come home bouncing off the walls. To sleep, I'd wash it all down with whatever flavored vodka seemed cool that day. I'd wake up starving and do it all again.

People noticed. I was fine. People reached out. I was still fine. People were scared. I was fine, and they were crazy. I lasted eleven months. My erratic behavior, fueled by destructive methods to survive that schedule, mercilessly cost me that position before my heart exploded. Looking back, I can't believe I made it that long. There was plenty left for me to learn, and morning wake-ups that early, where you're called to be not only coherent but entertaining, are still incredibly difficult. But with gratitude, a better understanding of happiness, and the right support system, thankfully, the Devil hasn't shown up again.

XVI • The Tower

The Tower shows up when an 'unexpected' turn of events rips through the fabric of familiar cloth that insulates your little world. You're shaken, you're shocked, and yet somehow, when you finally look in the mirror to check for invisible damage, the first thing you say to yourself is, "I should have seen this coming. *How could I not have seen this coming?*"

Have you ever wanted something so badly that you tricked yourself into thinking you had it? What happens when that illusion shatters? That moment—that's The Tower.

When I think of this card, it brings to mind the haunting crooning of Freddie Mercury on the 1991 ballad "The Show Must Go On," off of Queen's powerful *Innuendo* album. At the time, Freddie was battling the merciless effects of HIV/AIDS, and the end was near. Despite countless warnings about the harshness of the disease, many people in the mid to late '80s refused to compromise their hedonistic lifestyles in exchange for caution. By the time Freddie sang of the emptiness and isolation the narrator is experiencing throughout the lyrics of the song, Freddie's days on this planet were almost over. Queen would never tour again, and soon the world would be mourning the loss of one of rock and roll's most flamboyant frontmen. The irony of the entire situation is that Freddie's passing only seemed to strengthen the band's popularity. A nationally televised tribute concert and a renewed interest in the band's music helped Queen carry on, even until this day—albeit with different singers, and a slightly different look—with the same sense of purpose that they had since they arrived in the early '70s. When The Tower shows up, it can be cruel, and it can be unforgiving. But as Freddie sang in his goodbye to us on "The Show Must Go On," we will find a way to continue.

I mentioned a brief fling I had with a married woman. No, it was not my proudest moment. To be fair, it was a common-law thing, not an actual legal union, and she became much more 'married' as we started to actually date. It was stupid. I was stupid, and I knew better. However, I was avoiding the much bigger responsibility of ending my own shattered marriage in a dignified way. It was over; she had moved out, but I was still surrounded by my ex's belongings and hadn't yet begun to address who got what and how we would go about the paperwork. That's when I found myself submerged in a very unhealthy distraction.

For a moment, everything was great. I finally had someone in my life who understood me, who didn't make me feel like I was talking to an extravagantly decorated wall. During this massive change, I'd also fulfilled my dream of writing a song. Not just any song, but a song featuring three of my all-time favorite singers. The song had just been mastered, and the engineer waived payment because it was a song that targeted suicide prevention. The ratings for my morning show were once again on top, and I had a giant apartment all to myself where this new chapter of my life was firing on all cylinders. Like a fool, I looked at this paradise, swaying back and forth on a house of cards during a Category 5 storm, and felt like things were going *awesome*. I was on top of the world.

Within a month, the girl I suspended reality with went back to her husband and informed me via a text message, no less. Then my close friend, who starred in the music video for my suicide prevention charity single, tragically took her own life, effectively ending any plans to make it the global phenomenon I had envisioned. On top of all that, my program director and I got into a massive argument that lasted about two years, and my ratings suffered drastically in part due to the tension and lack of communication in the building. Finally, my beautiful apartment flooded, twice, ruining much more than my sneakers, clothes, and vinyl. Within just a few months, The Tower had shown up and fallen right on top of my little charade. It would all work out to be a much better life than I had then, but at the time, everything just fell apart.

XVII • The Star

Do you remember a time when a sliver of optimism shined through an extended period of darkness? Can you recall a moment when hope finally, mercifully, and perhaps miraculously prevailed? What happened that brought you to that moment?

When I first heard the Scorpions' "Wind Of Change" off of 1990's *Crazy World* album, it was the way most twelve-year-olds back then got introduced to new music—through the video on MTV. Many of my music fan friends talk fondly of how that soulful whistling, which leads into a powerful story of how the Soviet Union crumbled instantaneously, grabbed their attention. It grabbed mine, too. My first thought was, *Who is this dork, and why is he trying to be Axl Rose? Only Axl can whistle on a song.* I didn't have the patience to understand not only music history, but world history. I was too young to understand why a German-born band like the Scorpions cared about the fall of the Berlin Wall and what the end of the Cold War would mean to millions of people desperate for economic reform, societal change, and a new world where hope was now possible.

The Star comes after The Tower. You now have a clean slate to build upon. Every dream you ever had is now ready to manifest through the work and effort you are ready to put forth. Your heart is once again ready to give and receive. Your soul is ready to glow.

The pandemic isn't something any of us needs to revisit. Your life was turned upside down just as mine was. Whatever that life was, it was different for quite a while. At the start of it, I wound up quarantined with a new girlfriend and her two-year-old child. For the next few months, my life consisted of walking into an empty radio studio, doing a show for those who were out there helping everybody else, stopping for my zucchini pancakes from the supermarket, and then watching the same *Paw Patrol* DVD with a potty-training toddler. This was not even a full year from the events I discussed while looking at The Tower. This wasn't my plan, just as your life during that period of 2020 wasn't yours.

By November of that year, I was back home and single, and I began to open back up very slowly in sync with the rest of New York. I had just broken down and accepted my role as a lightworker that September. I flew to Florida with a mask on, listened to my mother's *I told you so 's* with acceptance, and flew back home with my first deck of Tarot cards. By November of 2020, I was slowly beginning to make sense of the last eighteen tumultuous months and was finally appreciative of what I did have. A career, friends, and a new outlook on a psychic world I'd never given a chance before.

My station, 94.3 The Shark, was getting ready for its first-ever mental health telethon called *Hope Rocks*, which featured a simple message: "With Music, You're Never Alone." I was strong enough to be excited for the first time since my world shattered in 2019. One morning leading up to the broadcast, I was live on air asking listeners for inspirational songs that pull them out of a funk. A few minutes later, my Instagram DMs were loaded with an expansive playlist from Nicole in Centereach. Turns out, Nicole was a brand new listener, stuck in a horrible traffic jam caused by a four-car pileup, and turned me on, hoping the tattooed big mouth would shut up long enough to give a current report on the road conditions.

That one moment of sharing on social media led to a wild conversation about Adam West's *Batman* and the obnoxiousness of yellow cars. That conversation led to a first date. A *date*! What the fuck was I doing on a date? With the *mess* I cause people? Well, after the understanding of many things that learning Tarot had afforded me, and the worst of the COVID lockdowns finally behind us, I walked into that bar, with nothing to lose, to meet the sassy music fan. I was emerging out of the ashes of the worst volcanic eruption I'd ever experienced, so to speak, let alone witnessed. The worst was behind me, with lessons learned and a chance to make much better decisions. More on that later...

Today, in 2025, Nicole is much more than a part of my life. She is my partner in Rock'n Soul Tarot, in our home, in my life. And it was all because I was finally in a place to let her in.

XVIII • The Moon

So, who exactly are you fooling? Are you trying to convince others of this "reality" you've created? What is it you claim to see? Now, ask yourself who is actually benefiting from your little distortion of the truth? How long can you keep up this angle?

Bruce Springsteen was my first superhero. Everything he wrote was my new favorite song. What the fuck a six-year-old knew about the struggles of working-class America, I have no idea. What a nine-year-old understood about a song that's about realizing how everything you thought you could offer someone turned out to be well beyond your reach is even more baffling. But "Brilliant Disguise" became one of my favorite songs since the day the Boss released it on 1987's *Tunnel of Love* album. This song is sung from the perspective of someone who feels they failed in their half of their promise of partnership. And yet, somehow, as the song unfolds, you get the sense that whoever he's singing this heartbreaking admission to is having a very similar internal battle—almost as if their own guilt is blinding them to the idea that there is more to the story than their own deceptive behavior.

Radio is a very cutthroat industry. In any one market, there are only a handful of on-air positions, and if someone is already behind that microphone, none of them are available. People are always looking to dethrone you, even those inspired by you, while at the same time seeking your advice. If you're adult enough to accept that, friendships are fairly common, just as long as you're not looking for anything beneath the surface.

With that understanding, out on the street you are perpetually cautious of anyone you meet. Every friendly listener seems like a good-hearted person who wants to tell you what you mean to them—until the next sentence, when they're demanding Foo Fighters tickets. Every "loyal listener" is usually the first to send an email calling for your head because you held them to the same set of rules everyone else has to follow, and you didn't just hand them the day's prize. Don't even dare run out of T-shirts at an event. That usually turns "I listen to you every day" into "I drove all the way out here, and you're not gonna hook me up? I will never listen again!"

Like any other dysfunctional relationship, these threats usually prove to be empty, but it's interesting to be a part of what they call "love." You do have an obligation to those who keep you employed, and I never recommend being outright rude. There is just always a little bit of mystery in how a listener truly feels.

Every year, I host a birthday party with special guest musicians and open up the event to my listeners. All of the money raised goes to Angela's House, a local Long Island charity that helps medically fragile children. The vibe in the air each year is intoxicatingly positive. Most people come to support the kids and share a drink with me, and it's a great time for all. I try to hang out with as many people as possible and show my appreciation, but it can be hectic as I get pulled in nineteen directions at once.

A few years ago, a couple came up to me in the midst of the chaos and handed me a signed New York Rangers puck. As a diehard fan of the team, I thought this was the sweetest gesture. They spent a few minutes explaining how much their morning commute had improved since I started coming along for the ride, and I actually got choked up. It was so heartfelt that I lost any suspicion that a request for concert tickets or a demand that I play their cousin's ska/polka fusion band on my heavy rock station disappeared. And, luckily, no such request ever came. It looked as if they were simply nice people doing a nice thing for someone they appreciated. All they asked for was a picture, which I gladly took with them.

About a year later, I got a message from an old intern of mine who probably hadn't contacted me in over a decade, so the alarms were already sounding in my head. He was a super nice kid, but he lived an extremely flamboyant lifestyle, while I chose a quieter, more conservative approach. So, once he left radio, we just didn't have much to talk about. Suspecting my surprise at his appearance, he wasted no time explaining what prompted him to reach out. He said he'd been scrolling through an LGBTQ friendly swingers website, and there *I* was. My picture. The one I took with the awesome couple who simply wanted to give me a little gift for my birthday.

The caption underneath the photo said, "We're looking for fun people to play with." We, as in them... and me! That sweet couple. Using my pic to bait others on a hook-up site within the LGBTQ community, which I have no problem with, by the way, but am not a part of. (At least the last time I checked.) Turns out, there was more to that sweet couple's story and motive after all.

XIX • The Sun

Would you understand the value of miracles if you experienced them daily? When you're around positive people, do you leave the conversation feeling more positive? Now, think about what your vibe is like after an hour with a negative Nancy? There is a reason why The Sun comes up so late in the major arcana, and just a few cards after The Tower.

There is probably a great argument to be had over what George Harrison's greatest song is as a Beatle. You would be dead wrong if your answer were anything other than "Here Comes the Sun." But you have your reasons, and I'm cool with it. The appreciation in Harrison's voice as he sees the sun starting to peer through the clouds is directly after what he describes as an isolating and brutal winter season. It's after he suffered through a dark period that he is able to find such a passionate appreciation for a metaphorical giant yellow thing in the sky. The message in the song is simple. The worst is over, now you can begin to enjoy what's coming.

My first few years at 94.3 The Shark were incredibly exciting. To be honest, the day this job stops being exciting is the day I am no longer the guy for the job. But back then, it was new and it was big and it was everything I worked for. It took a while to realize the abuse that the staff was enduring at the hands of the program director. You laughed it off when he made you the butt end of jokes on the air. He'd call me fat and point to my dad bod, all the while my mother was still on the Island listening. I would be subjected to 2 a.m. phone calls because I posted too many articles about wrestling and UFC, and then again at 2:30 a.m. because I liked a post the general manager put up on Facebook, and we weren't supposed to like him.

Rob and I would be mandated to interview bands before station-sponsored concerts while the PD drank wine with the hired models on the company tab. This went on for years, worsening increasingly, yet remaining unnoticed. I didn't trust management, as they came in during a merger and didn't seem like they cared enough, so I kept it to myself. I had my suspicions about the erratic behavior of my PD, but it didn't seem like anyone gave a damn. So, each time he demanded we meet him at this restaurant to talk "away from them," only to watch us eat while his full meal sat untouched on his plate, I said nothing. I laughed off every threat to stay away from certain hired models. He'd address any mistakes I made for an entire month, all in one tirade, and I'd just stand there and take it. Until that is, it all got to be too much.

One day, I walked into the GM's office, resignation letter in hand, when he asked me to sit down. Surrounded by the GM and the OM, I figured I was about to lose my job, which didn't seem all that bad at the moment. Instead, they gently broke the news that they'd fired the abusive PD. You know that weird feeling when you're expecting someone to say one thing, and what's said is so unexpected that you're not sure if you heard them correctly? That's how I felt in this moment. He was gone. Turns out, I wasn't the only one he was out of control with. But in today's lawsuit-driven world, no one was exactly sure what to say or do, and no one spoke up about their experiences with the abusive PD until he got so out of control that he started going after the higher-ups.

What actually happened, I don't know. But he was gone, and that's all that mattered. The two years that followed were honestly some of the happiest I had in that building. I became a part of the operation instead of a piece of it, if that makes sense. I looked forward to going to work each morning, even if my alarm still went off at 3:30 a.m. I began to appreciate being a morning show host again and learned things about the position that I'd never had the chance to notice before.

The darkness had ended. Light began to shine. And because I walked through the worst of it, I was able to enjoy The Sun that much more.

XX • Judgement

What have you gone through to get here? Your experiences. Think about the decisions you made to create them. There is a tricky question that Judgement challenges you to answer. How can your past actions determine your future circumstances?

When Judgement shows up, you are close to entering a new chapter. When a new chapter unfurls, you have to make peace with the last chapter, and you, the author, must dot all the i's and cross all the t's on the lessons you have already experienced. If you don't, the new chapter won't even be a sequel, just a printing error. The new chapter will simply be a reprint of the previous one.

Pat Benatar released a song on 1987's *Wide Awake in Dreamland* album that could serve as the mantra that the characters shown to be accepting their fate on the Judgement card sing back to the trumpet player emerging from the clouds. The song is "All Fired Up." In this very '80s-sounding pop rocker, the Long Island, NY, native sings about holding on to the belief that everything will unfold the way it's supposed to. She says that as long as you stay true to the plan within the boundaries set by the universe, it will all play out to a respectable and acceptable outcome. If you have truly played by the rules, this next step in life should prove favorable. However, if you're the only one who believes you've held a respectable standard, chances are you won't like the results, and once again, you'll have to be open to learning the lesson.

I have a big mouth. A big mouth and a short fuse that's coupled with a refusal to back down when I know I am right. That may sound noble, but it's cost me quite a few jobs throughout life, not to mention relationships, friendships, and a shot at being president of the Yogurt of the Month Club. Even if that last claim is a lie, the rest of that statement is all too painfully true. Being right has usually meant more to me than doing right.

I knew an old PD who was horribly out of touch with what classic rock radio was in the early 2010s. At the time, Alice In Chains, Soundgarden, and Stone Temple Pilots were more than two decades old, but we were still playing stuff from the mid-'60s. That's exactly the crowd we drew, which was to say, not much of one, since everyone seemed to be asleep after the early bird special. Despite our ratings continuing to tank, our summer grand prize winner being 79, and the answer to correcting it all being painfully obvious, this particular boss wouldn't budge. To him, "Classic Rock" was bands that played the original Woodstock, and that was that. His only exception seemed to be bands that played at The Last Supper.

Now, he was the boss, and there was probably a much gentler way to go about telling him his radio programming sucked, but I hadn't yet learned restraint. I was right, and I knew I was right, and he and everybody else were going to know it. I continued to argue my point even as I was being shown the door and my belongings were being tossed to the curb. That heritage rock station only withstood one more year of incompetent management before it was stripped of its rock format and repurposed as a political talk station, which proved me absolutely correct all along. Not that it made a difference, since I was still out of a job. I needed to learn to keep my mouth shut.

Years later, I was enjoying a successful run as the morning show host of a rock station that was almost *exactly* like the one I argued for a decade prior. Well, one day I was called into the GM's office and had the ultimate test placed upon me. I was being accused of making heinous threats to a local business owner. In an email that I will maintain until my dying breath was filled with lies, it was stated that I promised to respond to a disagreement over the phone by launching an on-air smear campaign designed to ruin the business owner financially and professionally. He went as far as to claim that he, a former law enforcement official, feared for his well-being because of the tone used with him by this forty-six-year-old with two bad hips and a busted shoulder. This was in response to him not holding up his end of a promise during a volunteer event I donated time to. Under no circumstances did I make such threats or even raise my voice. Radio is the only thing I ever took seriously, and I have never used it as a weapon. The entire accusation was ridiculous. Yes, I was stern with him. But threatening? No. Not even close.

But here I was, surrounded by my GM and OM, being forced to tell "my side of the story." There was no side. The whole thing was just a bunch of bullshit, but the GM seemed convinced that I had done these things. So I had a choice. Call him a fucking idiot for thinking I would ruin the one thing I was ever good at, or sit there and take it. I realized right there I wasn't gonna win this argument. In my mind, my GM was being an idiot, but what was the point in saying it? He didn't seem like the type to suddenly have an epiphany and tell me that "yes, yes, you're right." So I just sat there. I even smiled.

In my head, I said, "You wanna think I'm being an idiot? Okay, then do something about it." But there was no need to. I was a single person, a morning show host. There was no producer, no phone screener, no help. In an age where so many people work from home, I still come in every single morning, despite my limp getting noticeably worse and the pain that goes along with it becoming more aggravating by the day. For that time being, I recognized their need for me as much as mine for them. As upset as I was and as much as I wanted to tell this guy to go fuck himself, I chose to stay quiet. I simply walked away and had a decent weekend. By Monday, the GM had informed me that he'd called the guy and smoothed it over. I didn't respond to the email with anything more than "Thank you."

There was a part in there where my GM suggested I call the business owner to apologize. He looked pretty blue for weeks after that, so I wonder if he had held his breath after that request. I had much better judgment at forty-six, but judgment doesn't mean you have to lose your spine. Once I let it go, it didn't cross my mind again until it was time to write about Judgement. Great lesson.

XXI • The World

So, what do you consider to be the next level? Can you picture what it's gonna look like when you achieve it? When you look back to examine the journey so far, can you imagine what your rearview mirror will reflect back to you? When you get to the point when you can laugh at your past tragedies, that's when The World is upon you.

There is a line in Bruce Springsteen's crowd favorite "Rosalita" where, after he explains to his love interest that although he has accepted and understands her parents' disdain for his rock band profession, he is certain that his recent success with the label will surely change their minds. Soon, he muses, all of the hardships the young couple faced from their disapproving parents will seem funny. The harsh words and tense conversations won't simply vanish from the history books, but it just won't matter anymore, as everyone will be on to bigger and better things. The cycle has been completed, and a better one awaits. The old one? Well, that's just a memory to look back on and appreciate now in a way you couldn't then.

My wedding to my second wife was like a storybook fable that came to life. Family members came together for the first time in years. My brothers were finally all in the same room, my favorite band since I was fifteen played our wedding song, and everything went according to plan. It was perfect, which is why I should have known better.

My then-wife and I were still relishing in the glow of our successful union when we decided to explore the local shops of downtown Port Jefferson. Since our honeymoon wasn't until later in the week, we took some money from our wedding cards and decided to do what any responsible young couple would do—spend it on clothes and ice cream. Port Jeff is a Long Island town that's rife with Revolutionary War history and also carries a very strong metaphysical vibe. There are at least four crystal shops and a Masonic Hall within a few blocks of each other.

While walking hand in hand with my new bride, a corner shop jumped right out at me. Keep in mind, this was a few years before I touched a Tarot card for any reason other than handing them to my mother. For some reason I couldn't understand at the time, the Port Jeff Salt Cave stood out to me. I wasn't exactly sure what a salt cave was or why I would want to waste an hour in there, but it sounded cool. I suggested we take eighty bucks out of the $2,000 we had on us from the wedding and explore something new together. *No*, was the response I got. Too expensive. Looking back, it probably just didn't interest her, but there was something about not going into that little shop that left me very disappointed.

Eighteen months later, my second marriage was over. And despite the rumors, replicated oceanic environments had nothing to do with our vows being shattered in a year and a half. It just ended. A lot of unfortunate circumstances seemed to rain down on us, to the point where even a non-believer like me started to feel that the universe was telling us something.

Less than two years after that second divorce, I had met Nicole. Just two months prior to that, I had finally admitted to my mother that she was right. I was embracing my intuitive nature and took a deck of her cards to call my own. For a first date, in the middle of a flood of changes that included work personnel, a new apartment and loss, along with my psychic journey, Nicole suggested we walk around downtown Port Jefferson. I didn't think much about it. It wasn't like my previous marriage had the territory locked down. I had been hanging out for fun in Port Jeff since I was a teenager, and it was supposed to be warm on a New York November afternoon, so I said, "Why not?"

Now, as clichéd as it sounds, it sure as heck didn't feel like a first date. It felt like a reunion. We seemed so familiar to each other, and as much as it felt as if we had "been here before," we had this shared excitement about "revisiting" these moments.

Hand in hand, we laughed as we strolled across Main Street. Suddenly, Nicole stopped and pointed across the street. "Hey," she said excitedly, "do you think maybe we can go in there together?" It was the Salt Cave. She was pointing directly at the fucking Port Jeff Salt Cave. Without a second to think about it, I was led across the double yellow line and into this mysterious cave stuffed with thousands of pounds of Himalayan sea salt. Marcy, the owner, welcomed us with a huge smile and a hug— they hug a lot there—and within minutes, I was challenged. "Why aren't you using your gifts?" she asked. Keep in mind that, at this particular moment, she didn't even know my last name. "Why aren't you reading more?" she pressed on.

Now, instead of boring you with my litany of excuses and bullshit, I can honestly say that it was at *that* moment when I made a little but significant change and began a new chapter of my life. That's when my metaphysical journey began. Within a year, studying under Marcy evolved into me having a residency reading professionally at the salt cave, and it eventually became the home of my first psychic medium gallery. People were actually coming to watch me read other people. No pressure. I now teach at the salt cave as well.

I owe a lot of where I am now to those lessons I learned inside the Port Jeff Salt Cave with Marcy. Instead of walking past it again, I had listened to instinct, and Nicole, and walked inside.

Interlude

Brian Orlando came through my doorway with his then-girlfriend Nicole, who would become the great love of his life, one fateful afternoon at The Healing Center at Port Jeff Salt Cave. There was something immediately familiar about his presence.

We chatted a few times before Brian invited me to be a guest on his morning radio show, along with a well-known and respected Long Island psychic medium. I was there in the capacity of an intuitive numerologist. I was invited to calculate and read Brian's life path number for the show. I immediately knew there was so much more to this man than met the eye. I also immediately knew he was playing small.

I invited him to come and have a full soul plan numerology chart done at the Salt Cave. There we discovered—or, should I say, uncovered very quickly during his reading—all of his many psychic gifts, as well as a much larger audience for him than just radio. It took some prompting/nudging/nagging, but Brian has opened up to his gifts in a tremendous way. The rest, as they say, is history.

I am so humbled to be a small part of his amazing story.

— Marcy Guzman, The Healing Center at Port Jeff Salt Cave

Minor Arcana

Pentacles

ACE

What does 'free will' mean to you? What would you do with an offer so good you couldn't refuse it? Would you accept it without much thought? Or would you think yourself into a circular frenzy as the offer fizzled away?

Song to Help You Understand: "Into the Great Wide Open" — Tom Petty

The most important part of the song is how open-ended Petty leaves each verse, let alone the ending of the song. Even after the record label representative was left unimpressed with the results of the main character's recording session, to the point where he questions the commercial appeal of all of that hard work, the fate of the musician still seems to be in his own hands. He now has even more information about what he needs to do, and nothing truly seems to be blocking him.

It's up to you. The light is green. The path is clear. Nothing is stopping you. Be grateful. Be driven. Be ready.

TWO

Can your goals be achieved at your current pace? Are other areas of your life suffering because business is your only priority? Is your dedication to the cause worth what you may lose because of it?

Song to Help You Understand: "Fly from the Inside" — Shinedown

Brent Smith starts this song out by presenting his burden. He even makes sure to repeat himself, so there is no confusion as to the weight of the responsibility he is carrying. Because of this, he lets us know that he has no time for anything else. He lets us know that this isn't about right or wrong, or even who may feel one way about it or the other. His only focus is completing what he feels is his mission.

There is a time and a place to prioritize money, business, and goals. Is this that time?

THREE

If you are an electrician hired to help build a new house, are you installing the toilet bowl? If you are a jiu jitsu master, are you qualified to teach boxing?

Song to Help You Understand: "Ebony and Ivory" — Stevie Wonder and Paul McCartney

Though the title is self-explanatory, the premise can be applied to any two people with common hopes, dreams, and goals of peace, love, and financial security. This song calls you to listen, to learn, and to realize that we're a lot less different than we might have initially thought. Once you realize that everyone has something to teach you, it's a better environment to be in.

Partnership: the missing piece to the puzzle. A mutual understanding of a goal or project.

FOUR

Is it worth your sanity? Is it worth your health? Remember ... you can't take it with you.

Song to Help You Understand: "Tattooed Millionaire" — Bruce Dickinson

Iron Maiden was never a glamorous band. They were a heavy metal band with a purpose. The glitz, glamour, and decadence of 1980s "hair metal" didn't exactly fit who Iron Maiden represented themselves to be. Even after Bruce Dickinson embarked on a solo project, he remained a hard-nosed, no-nonsense rocker who sang about morals, traditions, and representing the importance of rock and roll music. "Tattooed

Millionaire" is the title track of a 1990 album that was released during an era that had already begun to denounce the excess of glam rock and called for things to be stripped back to the basics. Dickenson proudly admits to not needing all of the excess of his contemporaries' lifestyles. He no longer even needs Iron Maiden, a juggernaut in the industry, to be happy. He just needs a few guitars, a bass, and drums and to be left to his own devices.

This is when you realize what you always thought you wanted may not be what you need.

FIVE

Are you so sad and depressed that you just can't see the help that's in front of you?

Song to Help You Understand: "Leave a Light On" — Papa Roach

Jacoby and the band did a private concert for The Shark in 2024 for a mental health awareness organization. With all of the massive hits Papa Roach had put out over the years, it was "Leave a Light On" that the people at the event sang the loudest—a song that was just about two years old at the time. Tears were shed, vocal cords were strained, and strangers stood arm-in-arm with one another singing words that seemed to have been with them all of their lives. When Jacoby lets you know that he understands your pain—and understands it enough to know that he won't insult you by telling you it's gonna be okay, because he gets that you're not in a position to hear it—you respect his sentiment instantly. When someone tells you that they will be there when *you're* ready, it's an amazing way for them to express that they truly know what you're going through, and that they're willing and able to help when you're ready to accept it.

It's not as bad as it seems. You are not as alone as you feel. Help is within reach. And if you wipe the tears from your eyes, that help is within your sightline.

SIX

Who is that person you drop everything for? Are *you* that person?

Song to Help You Understand: "This is the World Calling" — Bob Geldof

It's a simple song about a complicated problem. Perhaps the solution to the complication is simple: Help. Help someone. What little you can do is a lot to someone in need. If everyone helped someone, everyone would get some help. Sometimes, we all just need a little. Bob Geldof calls out to *you* in this song. We all have it to give, and we all need it, too. Open your arms, open your heart, and accept it.

A loan. A place to stay. A job. An offer to get on your feet.

SEVEN

Can you stay focused when there isn't much of a result happening yet? Can you be patient when the work you're putting in has yet to reveal the payoff?

Song to Help You Understand: "God Gave Rock and Roll to You II" — Kiss

Kiss didn't start out as the biggest rock and roll band in the world. They had wicked humble beginnings playing to small clubs for feeble payouts. Even by the time they released their reworking of this 1973 Argent classic in 1991, the members of Kiss seemed to remember the early days. The song serves as a pep talk to those with big dreams. Big dreams require big work and an even bigger capacity for patience. There seems to be a whole lot of nothing happening on the way to the top, but while you see stagnation on the surface, the universe is working behind the scenes for those who stay the course and stick to the plan.

Slow to yield results — hard work now, but it pays off later.

EIGHT

What is the highest title you can earn right now? If you're a great at-home cook, what will it take to work in a bar, kitchen, or restaurant? If you're a cook, what will it take to become a chef?

Song to Help You Understand: "A New Level" — Pantera

In this song, Phil is sick of the world's bullshit, and he isn't gonna take it anymore. He demands you step up and be better. He dares you to let go of the losses and start lunging at the wins, to rise above what's holding you down by accepting that there is more—and you deserve more. This isn't a debate. It's a statement.

You have what it takes to level up. You have the knowledge and experience to now learn at that higher level. Do it.

NINE

Have you ever been so focused on the road ahead that you missed out on appreciating what you've already accomplished?

Song to Help You Understand: "Highway to Hell" — AC/DC

When Bon Scott sings his celebratory lyrics, never does he say that he's in a number-one-selling band. He simply says he is having a blast making it. The narrator never acknowledges that the flag was captured, but with that iconic riff and those simple but effective lyrics, we can all have some fun before the final victory. AC/DC makes it clear that they aren't waiting for the main goal to be accomplished before they start celebrating. They're having a *lot* of fun the entire time they're getting there.

For now, forget about what you're striving for and take a moment to celebrate how far you've come.

TEN

What's left to prove? If the answer is nothing, we are facing the Ten of Pentacles.

Song to Help You Understand: "Nothing Else Matters" — Metallica

This song is a ballad. Not like their older work, which were just slowed-down versions of their thrash master pieces, still laced with dizzying guitar solos. This sleeper off of 1991's *Black* album was a full-blown *ballad*. They cut their hair. They wrote radio-friendly compositions. They sold out! Their early fans, who considered themselves outcasts, were furious as the band embraced elements of mainstream musical properties and made music that was more widely accepted. The band's feelings about it seem to be obvious, as the song title itself pretty much puts it out there in neon lights. They *did* everything. They gave the world a heavy metal revolution. Now, it's about them. This song isn't as much of an apology as it is a proud declaration. They'd earned the position they were in and the room to operate so freely within it.

You have what you want. You act like you've been there before because you have. The Ten of Pentacles is the maturity and appreciation of that revelation.

PAGE

When did you realize money was important? That a career was important?

Song to Help You Understand: "Comedown" — Bush

Gavin never says how long it took him to realize what was important to him. But now that he recognizes he's on top of the world, every confusing arc of the journey suddenly makes sense. He never seems to forget what it took to get to the top, and because of that, he isn't planning on leaving his perch anytime soon.

Vision and enthusiasm carry you through the lack of experience. It's the beginning. Enjoy the newness.

KNIGHT

Are you annoyed by the attitude of risk takers? Are you the first to say "stick to the plan" when others get restless?

Song to Help You Understand: "Waiting" — Green Day

Billie Joe makes it clear in this song: He's close. He mentions the sentiment of gratitude more than once, and warns you to be ready for when your dreams finally come true. In other words, now is not the time to mess around, because you need to be ready. It seems as if he realizes that if he takes a shortcut now, he will be too focused on it to notice when what he's worked so hard for shows up.

It's the conservative approach. It may be boring, but it's the most trustworthy—and that's worth it right now.

QUEEN

Can you take care of your family, and the finances to support it, at the same time? Can you build a life where the focus is taking care of others, while still taking care of *you*?

Song to Help You Understand: "Both Sides Now" — Sammy Hagar

Sammy had left Van Halen by the time *Marching to Mars* was released in 1997. Sure, the crowds were large, but it wasn't Van Halen-sized audiences. The album made the top twenty, but it wasn't number one like his last collection of songs with VH. None of that seemed to matter, however, and Sammy seemed to tell us that in the lyrics to "Both Sides Now." He talks about fighting for a peaceful existence and facing darkness for brighter days. No, Sammy wasn't in one of rock's biggest bands in 1997, but through this song, he made it clear he had more than enough.

That work/life balance.

KING

Who comes to mind when you think of someone who always seems to understand how to make money? Who do you think of who always knows what to do?

Song to Help You Understand: "Winners Take All" — Quiet Riot

In this song, Kevin Dubrow is telling you how he got to be a best-selling band. He isn't really looking for advice or sympathy.

He doesn't even seem to care about praise. He's simply telling you how and why he is a winner. Since he's sharing, you might wanna stop and listen. The narrator in this anthemic ballad is letting you know that everything was worth it and that everything he did seemed to work out right in the end. The narrator of the song might be the person whose best-selling self-help book you buy.

A vision turned into a bona fide success.

A Note from Nicole

Brian connects with music, so he connects with people through music. Music is a memory, a feeling, air in your lungs, and a beat in your heart. It's a language and a lifestyle. It's a way back to yourself in a different time and place. It connects you to the faces and places of a certain time and place.

Brian is one of the most passionate and dedicated people I have ever met. He is generous and caring and grateful for every person he meets. It is a joy to watch Brian growing into the next chapter of himself—still the tattooed DJ with the backwards hat, but with a different type of awareness of the world around him, finding a new way to help and unite people.

Of all of the stories I could share with you about how the two of us connected over music, I will pick the following. When I met Brian, I asked him a slew of questions. It was my thing. You sure can tell a lot about a person based on their favorite '80s TV family, and whether they have ever seen the best movie in cinema history—Clue—and, not only have they seen it, but they can go line for line with you. We gave the TV families a "Top 3," and I had never met someone who could keep up with the movie lines as quickly as Brian could.

One of the questions Brian asked me was about my first concert. Well, that night, we uncovered that each of our first concerts was in fact the same show—The Beach Boys at Jones Beach in the '80s. We both went with our fathers. Both of our fathers are named John. They both have sisters named Donna. And their mothers were both named Jean.

I think during that specific conversation, we both knew that this, us, was something very different.

About a year after we started dating, Brian had tickets for us to see The Beach Boys at a popular intimate venue here on Long Island. We had seen dozens of shows together at this point. Getting to see the band from our first-ever concert, together, was one of the most kick-ass epic experiences. We sang every single song at the top of our lungs.

Our connection in the universe is now, but it has always been. And music is such an important part of the fabric that unites us.

Anyways, it's the best to sing so off-key and still have the hot guy with the backwards hat, tattoos, and killer smile want to sing along with you.

Wands

ACE

Have you ever asked for a sign that you were walking the right path, and it appeared? Did you ever just have that switch flipped and decide the time to act was now?

Song to Help You Understand: "Change" — Blind Melon

Shannon Hoon warns of complacency when he croons through the lyrics to track six on their 1992 debut album. He seems to understand that not everyone will accept his evolution, but he accepts that when all is said and done, most will see that it worked out for the best. The change Blind Melon sings about seems to come with a necessity rather than a curiosity.

This is spiritual. Possibly art/music/self-improvement based.

TWO

What's the plan? Are your ducks in a row? Is that a chicken? Ducks! Are you staying put or planning on something bigger?

Song to Help You Understand: "Tonight Tonight" — The Smashing Pumpkins

Billy Corgan recognizes that changing will cause you to leave older parts of you, parts that are no longer serving you, behind. And just because you aren't benefiting from them anymore, this doesn't mean you won't miss them. The Pumpkins seem confident that the change you *need* can be made tonight. Any night, as long as it's finally night. He acknowledges that the change may not be right, but staying put is wrong. So, believe that it's right and make a move.

Explore your options.

THREE

What are your self-perceived limitations? Can you dream bigger than them?

Song to Help You Understand: "It's My Life" — Bon Jovi

Jon Bon Jovi makes a big declaration at the beginning of this song that it's not for people who have given up, backed down, and just taken whatever shaft was aimed at them with a smile. This song is for the fighters, the believers, the ones who wouldn't let the doubts of others darken their light. If you remember Tommy and Gina from way back in 1987, they were on the verge of complete collapse when the band gave us "Living on a Prayer." We never found out within the song if they made it, but we understood that all they needed was their belief that each other's support would see them out of the lost woods. Thirteen years later, during 2000's "It's My Life," we still never find out how they got by, and that's okay. The song was dedicated to their tenacity and their refusal to stay where they were. They move along, despite the odds being against them. When Jon Bon Jovi declares that the time is *now*, he's talking from a place deep within.

Adventure. Exploration. Travel.

FOUR

Who has helped you get to where you are now? Who would remind you of everything you went through while making you laugh during stories of the hard times?

Song to Help You Understand: "It's Been a Long Time" — Southside Johnny and the Asbury Jukes

Little Steven Van Zandt wrote this for the Jukes' 1991 comeback album *Better Days*. The entire four minutes is a trip down memory lane, where the singer laments over days when the Jersey Shore was their bed, and there was just enough money for a single coat for a bunch of friends to share. Bruce

Springsteen joins both Johnny and Steven on these vocals, which ring out in appreciation of not only everything they have, but also what they went through to get to where they are now. We learn that not everyone made it, as they toast their fallen friends in each chorus. Springsteen is obviously the most recognizable of the trio on the song, but when you look to where they all started in the clubs of the Jersey Shore, it's easy to understand why all three had very good reasons to celebrate being together after over two decades of searching for their place in rock and roll history.

Celebrate each milestone. Make sure you appreciate who you're with.

FIVE

Are you being heard? Are you aware of who's not listening to you?

Song to Help You Understand: "Giants" — Sponge

The relationship we learn about in this song from 1994's *Rotting Piñata* isn't much of a relationship at all. It seems like most of the things done in this relationship aren't out of spite to harm the other, but simply to test if either of them even notices at this point. Lead singer Vinnie Dombroski wonders if his destructive behavior is on her radar while acknowledging her infidelity but only to wonder if she realizes that he found out. Despite the horrible behavior by both, they still seem to want the other to simply *see* them, hear them, and let the other one know they still exist in their world.

Let in other points of view. Bridge gaps in communication.

SIX

Who will cheer you at the halfway point? Who, right now, will want to hear all about the project, even though it's not complete yet?

Song to Help You Understand: "Bridge Over Troubled Water" — Simon and Garfunkel

The message of this 1970 folk classic is simple: No matter what part of the journey the narrator's friend is on at that moment, he will be there to help him through it. The lyrics not only mention darkness, but also moments where light will shine. And through it all, this song serves as a promise from one person to another to be there through everything.

Acknowledge what you've overcome. Recognize who will be there for the journey ahead of you.

SEVEN

Does what you have make you a target? Are you facing mounting pressure from your peers?

Song to Help You Understand: "I Won't Back Down" — Tom Petty

When the Seven of Wands is staring back at you, Tom Petty's 1989 anthem of defiance is what you might be playing in your head over and over again. The phrase about not backing down is constantly repeated to remind the narrator of his will to keep fighting. It is also a warning to those looking for the fight. This song serves as a war cry against those who are challenging your place at the top. The same message that screams out into the night as a warning to any who dares to FAFO (fuck around and find out) is also a gentle inner voice that's there to encourage you to stand your ground.

Defend. Stand your ground.

EIGHT

How many more signs do you need? How much longer are you going to wait before springing into action? What's left to play anyway?

Song to Help You Understand: "Change" — Candlebox

The first single off of Candlebox's debut album talks about how it's all been written out already, yet frustration is setting in because the story has yet to be completed. Lead singer Kevin Martin sings of things constantly getting complicated, maybe even confused, and it seems it's because there is too much talking happening and not enough action. Since it *has* been written already, all you have to do is go get it. The future is only in your hands if you reach out to grab it.

Move forward.

NINE

Are you really going to give up now? Has anyone ever told you to give up? Even if it was well-intentioned, how did you handle it?

Song to Help You Understand: "I'm Still Standing" — Elton John

This declaration in song form from 1983 starts out with the narrator telling the listener that they couldn't possibly understand his experiences and what it took to survive them. With that being said, there is no room for criticism or even advice, since there is no possible way to understand who and what you're coaching. At this stage in life, Elton John isn't looking for validation. The fact that he's still here, still going strong, seems to *be* that validation.

Shut out the noise.

TEN

Why are you doing so much? Is all of this extra effort helping you, your family, or your friends?

Song to Help You Understand: "Sometimes" — Candlebox

This is a somber ballad with a profound look into the reasons why we do more than we are supposed to. The weight that lead singer Kevin Martin is referring to seems to be the extra effort being added to his relationship in a last-minute attempt to keep it together. Sometimes we do more than what's asked or expected of us, and we challenge the concept of what's possible when the situation at hand proves to be extraordinary. All throughout the song, we are reminded that the heavy lifting is more than anything he imagined himself capable of. But as the song reminds us, these situations only arise "Sometimes."

A sick relative. An unreasonable amount of overtime to pay for a new house. The extra weight is temporary.

PAGE

Why are your feet still planted?

Song to Help You Understand: "Nothing's Gonna Stop Me Now" (*Perfect Strangers* theme song) — David Pomeranz

TV themes are catchy by design. They're supposed to command your attention from the opening note. The first few chords to the *Perfect Strangers* theme call to mind an early morning, the start of a new day, when you're immersed in optimism. Without seeing one minute of the actual sitcom, the image of Bronson Pinchot's Greek farmer character, Balki, waving goodbye to his family from the back of a dilapidated pick-up truck while clutching an "America or Bust Sign," lets us all know that *this* could be the day when change begins. It's such a radical move to give up a simple sharecropper's life on the property of a tiny foreign town that we all seem to forget that, moments earlier in the TV intro, Mark Linn Baker's character, Larry, had also just said his goodbyes to his American-suburban lifestyle to try his luck in the big city. We tend to look at things in extremes, and when anyone talks about this gem of an '80s sitcom, chances are you'll hear a plot line about a simple farmhand from another country who left everything behind to start a new life in America. We all seem to forget that cousin Larry left his safety net behind as well to try his hand at something greater than he'd previously experienced. Both men are standing tall as the momentum of finally stepping forward into their power is propelling them faster than the time they have to think about it.

Just because you're seeking help now doesn't mean you're not ready to move forward.

KNIGHT

Have you ever been so enamored with an adventure that you ignored the glaring warning signs? Have you ever been so focused on yourself that you never stopped to realize how others might be affected? Did it matter once you did?

Song to Help You Understand: "Anarchy in the UK" — Sex Pistols

It's easy to hear straight anger in Johnny Rotten's snarling delivery. With each declaration of "I *am*," he lets you know what you're dealing with in him, and he couldn't be less apologetic about it. If you soften just a bit to the lyrics, they can quickly evolve from a sentiment of anger to one of determination. This seems like the attitude that needs to be taken right now, in that moment. It's what the narrator of this song needs to survive, and one day to thrive. It's snotty, it's brash, and yet somehow it's charming.

Impulsive. Unapologetic.

QUEEN

Are you sure you're close? Are these feelings you're showing the ones you expected to have?

Song to Help You Understand: "Secret Garden" — Bruce Springsteen

The woman Bruce sings about has everything under control. She keeps everyone at a distance that she determines, despite whatever frustration her suitors might feel. If they get closer, more will come, and her precious boundaries and ideals will become compromised. Sounds admirable, until you dig under the surface and realize there isn't much more to her. Unlocking this woman's secret garden is a game that seems to render anyone capable of cracking the code hopelessly exhausted once that mission is accomplished. So what good is it to pursue this prize, and how much of a prize is she really?

You're not in control of your feelings. You're not as close as you think. You're masking an inner battle with outer strength.

KING

Can you look back on the experiences that crafted your vision?

Song to Help You Understand: "Don't Tell Me" — Van Halen

The narrator of this song isn't showing you his anger. He isn't getting into why he's walking down such a narrow road with little room for change or evolution. He's simply telling you that, based on what he saw, this is how he sees the world now, and this is how he's going to live his life—even if it means he won't have much of one. You may not agree with his choices, but they are his choices based on his experiences, so talking him out of them would be pointless.

There is no time for situations that don't lead to anything other than where you want to go.

A Note from John Hampson, Nine Days

Just how DID music connect Orlando and me? Obviously, we are geographically connected with us both being Long Islanders, but it was definitely music that brought us together in that "Dude!" manner that we cool cats have.

I'm a musician, and Orlando, among many other interesting things, is a Long Island rock star morning drive time DJ. So there's that. But I'm trying to remember how and when we initially got to know each other, and I can't. It feels like we've just been in each other's orbit for a couple of decades. He's a few years younger than I am, so he might've been sneaking into bars to see my band when I was in my early 20s, or we may have connected when he was DJing on the radio, or maybe it was through a mutual friend. Either way, it was music that brought us together and fostered the friendship that we share.

I do remember one particular moment when I think our connection sparked and really happened. Orlando was doing a segment for his radio show and asking artists what song really hit them emotionally—a song that they would listen to when they needed a lift. I told him there were two songs that I could almost never listen to without choking up: "Under Pressure," by Queen and David Bowie, and "Solsbury Hill," by Peter Gabriel. We talked a lot about those songs and those artists and how there was something absolutely magical and triumphant about them, even though they were addressing some of the difficult challenges we face.

I think that's when we went from polite appreciators of each other, music, and Long Island culture, and stepped into what has become a great friendship, one that's built on a mutual love and passion for music. We both get more out of songs and music than the average casual listener because we're digging in deep and letting the songs affect us emotionally and spiritually, without any self-conscious roadblocks. Just geeking out over "Under Pressure" and Freddie Mercury was a bonding moment.

At this point, we've been through many such conversations about music, including a bunch of radio interviews where we pretend to be professionals, all the while knowing what lucky knuckleheads we really are. We have even co-promoted and produced a live event that saw both of us digging deep into our pockets to save the show at the last second—it turned out amazing, by the way—because nothing was gonna get in the way of a great concert full of great music. That moment sealed our friendship. Where would we be without music?

Swords

ACE

Have you ever raised someone's confidence with a pep talk? Have you ever shattered someone's ego with brutal observations and honesty?

Song to Help You Understand: "Words as Weapons" — Seether

Shaun Morgan spends his time during this 2014 summer single searching for the correct reply to a poisonous dialogue. You get the sense that if he can just find the right phrase, the right collection of softer words, the volatile nature of the conversation will automatically lighten up. Whether he achieves this or not, you can see that he realizes just how powerful his words can be.

New missions. Communication. The mental power to withstand the trials and tribulations ahead.

TWO

Have you ever delayed a decision because you didn't like the possibilities of any potential outcome? Think back to a time when you pretended it was all okay because that was easier than the decisions you had to face if you admitted it wasn't.

Song to Help You Understand: "Should I Stay or Should I Go" — The Clash

Joe Strummer captures the pros and cons of a strenuous relationship perfectly here. As he explains to the person on the other side of the strained partnership, no matter what he does, there will be consequences. So, make up your mind and live with a decision already, before it becomes *just* a decision. He seems to want a decision to be made while there is still something to decide upon.

THREE

Can you look back at some hard lessons and rationally think about how they predicted the future? Do they come during happy times, or do these lessons become clear during or right after a struggle? Would you be as strong as you are now if everything in life went your way?

Song to Help You Understand: "Every Rose Has Its Thorn" — Poison

At the beginning of this classic MTV-era power ballad, the couple's relationship already seems strained beyond repair as the uncomfortable distance between them overcomes the energy in the room, despite them lying in the same bed together. By the end of the song, the woman has moved on with little remorse, while the male narrator is left wondering how he wound up with a shattered heart—yet it all comes back to the title of the song. The best part of everything has a bad part, and sometimes we draw the short straw to get that part. Analyzing it any further is just ripping even wider the wound the thorn has created. Once she finds a new partner in the final verse, there is no longer a reason to continue on with the song.

The news is harsh, bitter, and what's needed to move on.

FOUR

Have you ever won a serious battle, but still needed time to recover from it? Has fighting ever worn you down to the point where you just couldn't do it anymore?

Song to Help You Understand: "In My Tree" — Pearl Jam

Sometimes, looking at where a band was at the time a song was written gives you a better idea of what it's about than any 4 a.m., drunken rambling with your music nerd friends. By 1997, the buzz behind the Seattle music explosion had fizzled out. Kurt Cobain of Nirvana was gone, Layne Staley of Alice In Chains was crippled by personal demons, and Soundgarden had broken up. Pearl Jam was the last of the core four Seattle sons still intact, and they had just emerged from a highly publicized battle with Ticketmaster with a much less than favorable outcome. "In My Tree" seemed to tell the world where the band's head was after standing with their feet to the fire for more than half a decade. The song talks of a secluded place where newspaper headlines and shallow gossip cannot reach them, a place so far from the outside world that the only sound they can hear is their battle wounds healing.

You need rest to recover. Silence is golden. Inactivity is welcomed.

FIVE

Have you ever invoked that great verbal kill shot to rip someone's heart out—and then regretted it because you irreparably damaged your relationship? Do you regret going so hard at someone, even though you probably meant every word that came out of your mouth at the time?

Song to Help You Understand: "Living Years" — Mike and The Mechanics

The lyrics in this song explain why we say such horrible things sometimes. It doesn't apologize for caustic language hurled emotionally during fits of rage. It talks about how each piercing of the skin, each small battle lost, can build up in the back of your mind until, one day, it all bursts out onto someone who may have simply reminded you of all the pain and shame accidentally. Sometimes, we have lost so many small battles that when it's clear we have a chance to win one, we go more than a little overboard. By the end of the song, the narrator recognizes that these moments, where ego got in the way of the bigger picture, cost him something that no perfect insult can replace. The father of the main character in the song had passed away, so anything that could have been said, no longer can be.

Make sure what you're about to say is worth it.

SIX

Have you ever reached that point where the fear of what's ahead no longer scares you more than what you're desperate to leave behind? Has whatever seemed like a hard choice turned out to be a much easier ride than expected, once you finally got off your ass and moved forward?

Song to Help You Understand: "Land of Hope and Dreams" — Bruce Springsteen

It had been twelve long years since the E Street Band had toured together. Fans were starving. During that long hiatus, Bruce Springsteen had won Oscars, released solo acoustic projects, and seemed so far removed from the music his fans yearned for. There had already been a few false alarms of a reunion. So, at the end of the E United Tour of 1999–2000, when *it finally happened*, Bruce would end most shows with "Land of Hope and Dreams." In this song, there is no promise of mansions and golden paths. There is only a promise that there is a road ahead and the confidence that, this time, no matter what has happened before and who you've become, it's all gonna work out.

It doesn't look easy, but that's the beauty of this new chapter. Enjoy.

SEVEN

Ever do something you knew was dead wrong, but personal feelings wouldn't let you be honest about it? What caused you to finally stop?

Song to Help You Understand: "Illicit Affairs" — Taylor Swift

You can make fun of me all you want, but this chick can write. In this mournful ballad, she's admitting to how absolutely insane her secret rendezvous is while simultaneously making excuses for continuing to embarrass herself by continuing to lie, cheat, and fool around in some parking lot like a teen in heat. She's angry at herself for not having the discipline to end the destructive situation, but also at her questionable partner for not putting this thing out of its misery and saving her the anguish of making the decision.

Betrayal and cover-up.

EIGHT

Can you think clearly when you're panicked? Have you ever thought of a solution while flying into a fit of rage?

Song to Help You Understand: "Joey" — Concrete Blonde

Lead singer Johnette Napolitano didn't need to use actual words for us to feel her level of frustration. The person she was pleading with in this power-pop ballad from 1990 was destroying everything around him by simply giving in to his self-loathing and tearing himself apart. It seems as if the narrator in the song has finally realized that there is no breaking through to someone who holds himself in such contempt. There is no reaching someone who's that deep into drowning out their torment with self-inflicted physical and emotional mutilation. So, she gives in to her own feelings about it and simply promises herself—and him—that, if and when he's done being angry at the world, she will be there to pick him up and get him back on his feet. She isn't proud of her decision. She isn't happy about it. She just knows it's all that can be done at the moment. So she'll work on herself while he works through whatever demons are keeping him from hearing her.

Swallow your pride. Sacrifice. Accept that there is no easy way out.

NINE

Can you replace a negative thought with an equally positive one? Have you ever worried about something so much that your fear wound up rearing its ugly head? Were you right that it was gonna happen all along, or did you will the unwanted situation onto yourself?

Song to Help You Understand: "Get On Out" — Soul Asylum

Throughout this frantically paced rocker off of 1992's *Grave Dancers Union*, the lead singer peppers you with impossible-to-answer questions about the fate of his health, wealth, and love life—questions that would drive someone who's placed into the position of answering them far away, and fast. You can't help someone who won't believe that solutions are possible. You can't assure someone who refuses to look at any reasons for why they should put their fears to rest. As the narrator of this song is loudly declaring that he has to stop thinking so negatively, you get the sense that it's because there is no one left to listen to him.

Unhealthy fear. Irrational worry.

TEN

Have you ever wasted precious time being the victim instead of recovering from the crime? What can you learn from the loss?

Song to Help You Understand: "Backstreets" — Bruce Springsteen

No matter what happened between the narrator of this song and Terry, the love interest who deserted their vow to be together forever, the tone in Springsteen's voice makes you realize immediately that the pain inflicted by the break-up makes any chance at reconciliation impossible. He is hurt, betrayed, and disgusted at the thought of another man whisking her away. And yet, after forcing himself to experience every wave of emotion brought about by this ordeal, he agonizes all by himself at the end of the song that it is truly over. How it happened and why it happened no longer matter. His only way through the darkness is to come to terms with the fact that all that matters now is that he accepts the cold truth of the situation. She's never coming back, and there is nothing to come back to.

There is nothing left to do but move on.

PAGE

When have you learned the most valuable lessons? Have you ever experienced a sense of freedom when faced with the realization that there is nothing to lose by going for it?

Song to Help You Understand: "Dreams" — Van Halen

Van Halen was one of the biggest bands in the world when, in the blink of an eye, they no longer had David Lee Roth as their lead singer. Whatever expectations were laid out, the pressure of meeting them must have been astronomical. When Sammy Hagar sang the lyrics to "Dreams," with images of standing on top of shattered expectations of what could have been ringing out through the song, his understanding of the role as the new singer of one of rock and roll's greatest bands seems obvious. As Sammy's voice reaches a screeching pitch while singing of rising higher than he's ever had to, the only thing that seems to pierce through the fear in his voice is his excitement.

KNIGHT

Think of a time when you rushed into action on impulse, and the impulse paid off. Now think of a time when acting impulsively got you into trouble. In both circumstances, were you just sick and tired of the emptiness in other people's words about the situation, while nothing was being done about it?

Song to Help You Understand: "It's My Life" — The Plasmatics

The lead singer of the Plasmatics has a simple attitude throughout this entire song, which was written by Gene Simmons of Kiss, who has been unapologetic throughout his entire career. Win or lose, and whether you love or hate her, everything she does is hers and hers alone. She sounds tired of what others have to say, and rather than waste time trying to get anyone to see it her way, she's just going to take matters into her own hands. If you're smart enough to understand what she's doing, you'll probably enjoy it.

Action. Desperate for intellectual communication.

QUEEN

Have you ever been *too* truthful? Did you really need to say that to someone?

Song to Help You Understand: "Who's Gonna Ride Your Wild Horses" — U2

This underrated single off of 1991's *Achtung Baby* seems to be about loving the wrong person on a surface level. Yet, if you listen to what Bono despises about the situation, it isn't her characteristics but his attraction to them. This queen isn't interested in anyone who doesn't get it. Throughout the song, you hear about her actually giving the narrator the things he's asking for, but his inability to handle her way of doing it leaves him wounded.

Isolation is freedom if you 're not connecting.

KING

Have you ever heard the phrase *I'm just doing my job*? Think of a time you gushed over someone who reacted with this cliché. Now think of a time you were furious with someone who was just doing what they were supposed to do.

Song to Help You Understand: "Everyday Hero" — Smash Mouth

The concept is as simple as the energy of the card. You have an assignment, and you are going to carry out the assignment. Every hero mentioned in this song is just an ordinary human being tasked with a job that others might look at as extraordinary. Smash Mouth truly captures the essence of someone who has no time to marvel in the excitement of what they're doing. They're simply trying to make sure they're doing it the right way.

Authority, but fair. Someone to count on. A black-and-white take.

A Note from Jenny Crystals • Peace Love Prana, Shirley

Meeting Brian was a gift in itself. Not only is he a great friend and talented medium, but his selflessness is immeasurable.

From the first time I met him, he offered words of encouragement, and without looking for anything in return, he offered opportunities to help me grow my spiritual practice. He's a top-tier soul, definitely one of those light workers sent here to assist humanity in discovering their God-given abilities. He's an amazing teacher who created Rock 'n Soul Tarot, which demonstrates a beautifully unique way to help others understand the Tarot.

I have personally had enlightening conversations and incredible mediumship readings with him that have changed my course in such a positive way. His passion for organizing charities for causes dear to his heart is commendable. He is a multi-talented soul, and I'm honored to call him my friend.

Cups

ACE

Can you paint a picture of happiness in your mind? What is on that virtual canvas? When you're excited for the next chapter, what does that look like?

Song to Help You Understand: "Leap of Faith" — Bruce Springsteen

Something weird happened in the '90s: music got a lot darker. Grunge was at the forefront, representing the angst of a generation that was sick and tired of being told that everything was great. The representatives of '90s rock music wore the heaviness of rock star responsibility on the sleeve of each song and music video they released, warning us all that fame, fortune, and abundance came with responsibility that you may not want to handle. Meanwhile, in 1992, one of rock and roll's favorite sons, who made a *killing* during the '70s and '80s interpreting the plight of the struggling working-class American, went in the completely opposite direction. Bruce Springsteen was writing happy songs, with a brand-new band, from his hometown of New Jersey, 3,000 miles away from Los Angeles, as he embraced a radically different image of life. As new as it was to his fans, it was just as new to *him*, and that was startlingly clear on this song off the *Lucky Town* album. Gone was the E Street Band.

Nowhere to be found was a man questioning his faith in his safe, nine-to-five work environment. Bruce was happy? Bruce was excited? Bruce was telling us how great everything was? It was a strange time to be a fan, but for The Boss, it was a chance to evolve from his long-standing blue-collar image and embrace an adventure the young rebel rock star from Freehold, NJ, would never have thought possible as a teenager looking to make it in rock and roll. The fans never truly accepted his boyish excitement, but listening to a song that lays out just exactly how happy he was to leap into this new chapter of his life and career, it was hard not to be excited for him.

A time for giving. Radiating happiness.

TWO

Have you ever reached a new level in your career, relationship, or even hobbies, and thought to yourself, *Oh, man, this is big*?

Song to Help You Understand: "I'll Stand by You" — The Pretenders

Chrissy Hynde probably didn't mean to capture the energy of the Two of Cups perfectly. The serendipity in this universe is one of its natural wonders. The way to realize you truly care about someone you love, care about, and want to see succeed is to reach out to them and offer a hand. You may notice they need one, but how many times have you been caught up in your own struggles to notice anyone's good sentiments? The first thing The Pretenders' frontwoman asks when this song begins is why whoever she's talking to is wearing their emotions so outwardly. Perhaps she cares so much that it may not be that big of a deal to the person listening, but the Two of Cups isn't waiting for the shit to hit the fan to take action. Those who check in along the way, and not just at the finish line, are the type of people represented in this song, and with this card.

Don't wait until the wheels fall off for help. Celebrate as you grow.

THREE

Who are the friends that you trust to know where the bodies are buried? When you're asked about magical memories, who is in the story every time? When you talk about getting over a really rough time, who do you gush over helping you through it all?

Song to Help You Understand: "Here's to Us" — Halestorm

The celebration in this song seems to be a nod to being each other's ride or die. Lzzy Hale sings about wanting to toast someone, not because she's had a really rough couple of days, but to honor the person who is still standing there when she finally gets to the end of the week. It's implied that not much needs to be said between her and whoever she's singing to. Just one look from the other person is enough to know what is needed for the evening. If no one else can hang in this hour-long conversation, which consists of nothing more than sideways glances, sonic smirks, eye rolls, and giggles, then they can fuck off.

This is personal.

FOUR

Are you letting opportunity pass you by? What moments in life could be so traumatic that you are hiding in the dark so deeply that no light is reaching you?

Song to Help You Understand: "Indifference" — Pearl Jam

There is a lot of heaviness weighing down the mood of this ballad from Pearl Jam's sophomore album, *Vs.* The song brings to mind images of hurting yourself just to let the conscious mind know that you still feel. Meanwhile, Eddie Vedder continues to ask how much more he has to take—and how much more he's gonna take. In 1993, Pearl Jam was one of the biggest bands in the world, and their second album proved they weren't a fluke. Beneath all of this was a band riddled with scars. Pearl Jam had risen from the ashes of Mother Love Bone in 1990, when lead singer Andy Wood passed away just months before the band was about to lead Seattle into its cultural revolution. With a quarter-million-dollar advance from the record label, a planned tour with Aerosmith, and a fan base that was growing by the day, Mother Love Bone was heralded as the band to lead the Northwest music explosion to unseen heights. Then, it all fell apart with one error in judgment. For Stone Gossard and Jeff

Ament to pick themselves back up, put it all back together, and head into a new direction, all the while becoming one of the icons of their generation, is nothing short of astounding. Imagine the energy it must have taken. By 1993, Stone and Jeff had reached the second level of the top of Music Mountain, gotten unceremoniously thrown from it, rose even higher within their reinvention, and were now massive cogs in a machine responsible for making a lot of people a lot of money—all within three years. As breathtaking as the victory must have been, the battle to claim it had to be exhausting. The lyrics to "Indifference" seem to indicate that. Sometimes, after the storm, you need a little shelter.

You don't feel like you're in the shape to fight right now.

FIVE

Can you think of a moment in your life that still hurts, even months or years later, because it didn't turn out the way you thought it would?

Song to Help You Understand: "45" — Shinedown

Right before the chorus kicks in, Brent Smith realizes that he has held onto so much pain that it has aged him greatly, that he was wallowing in a traumatic episode for so long that he didn't realize how much time had passed by—and probably with a lot of new beginnings racing past him during those moments. He still cannot embrace change or even begin to understand how he can start to.

It's time to forgive yourself and let go of the weight holding you down.

SIX

When was life the most fun?

Song to Help You Understand: "No Surrender" — Bruce Springsteen

This is a song where Springsteen is looking back on his more innocent days, while relishing in what will soon become the pinnacle of his popularity in 1984, as the world was about to be introduced to the *Born in the U.S.A.* album. He is unapologetic about having no time for school as a teenager, still claiming to have found all the education he needed in his favorite bands' 45s and 33s. He talks about how good it felt to dream about rock and roll being more than just something outcasts did in the garage, and how the innocence of the dream was still something he can picture, even though he's long since been introduced to all of the realities of rock superstardom. By the time the *Born in the U.S.A.* tour started, the E Street Band was consistently playing stadiums that were bigger than they ever had before. Yet, The Boss was without his long-time best friend from the time he was sixteen. Miami Steve Van Zandt morphed into Little Steven to embark on an activist-driven solo career. On tour, "No Surrender" became a solo acoustic ballad, as Bruce reflected on a stage in a time when all of this success was just something his buddies talked about. It's not that he wasn't having fun being rock and roll's favorite son; it's just that he still had a fondness for a time when everything was less complicated.

Harkening back to a time of purity and simplicity.

SEVEN

Are you being realistic? Are you being honest with yourself?

Song to Help You Understand: "Through the Never" — Metallica

In the lyrics to this song, James Hetfield ponders the universe being big enough to carry secrets right in front of us. He questions the capacity to understand, as much as the *ability* to understand. Some things might be too big for us to grasp, yet we still have a responsibility to ourselves to think, plan, and move forward. How much we truly get right is a question for a later time, but making sure you're grounded before decisions are made seems to be a warning in this song, which is the theme to a heavy metal concept movie similar to Pink Floyd's *The Wall.*

Unrealistic ideas. A call to regain focus.

EIGHT

Has the story ever gotten so repetitive that you finally decided to stop rereading the same paragraphs? When in life did you finally realize that it just wasn't going to work out? How many times did it blow up in your face before you got the hint?

Song to Help You Understand: "Wake Up" — Mad Season

The lyrics to this song could be a conversation that the narrator is having with you as you struggle to come to terms with the lack of change in your life. The change is lacking because you are refusing to admit you need it. Another way to interpret the leadoff track to Mad Season's 1995 lone studio album is that this is your own inner voice letting you know that you cannot abuse yourself anymore. This could be not letting anyone else abuse you, or simply understanding that you can no longer maintain your status quo.

No more excuses. It's not working.

NINE

Have you ever looked around and thought, *Man, this is such a beautiful life*? As you said that, were you a millionaire? Was every bill paid? I once watched a very famous musician give a seminar, and at the end he said, "Nobody gets what they want when they need it." That stuck with me. How many coaches, bosses, and people who've had great influence over you said, "Act like you've been there before"?

Song to Help You Understand: "Danny's Song" — Loggins and Messina

It isn't wealth that causes this emotional outpouring. It isn't a fancy car that makes Kenny Loggins practically break down in happy tears during the chorus to this 1971 classic. It's what he already has—a bond with who he's singing to—that makes it more than enough to feel that it's enough. Sometimes, it's that simple. According to the narrator of "Danny's Song," the key is to be happy for what he has.

Look at what you already have. Be grateful.

TEN

Ever feel the need to just blow everything off that's work-related, because there are people in your life you need more right now than the raise, the pool, the car, and other material things? Have you ever looked at your family, friends, the people you trust, and thought, *I am one lucky human*?

Song to Help You Understand: "That's What Friends Are For" — Dionne Warwick and Friends

Only the '80s could have allowed this amount of corniness to be cool enough to be a number-one hit. The toughest, most rugged men have dropped their pool sticks and laid their darts on the table to drunkenly bellow these lyrics arm-in-arm with their "brothers," their "ride or dies," without a care in the world. This song is about friends promising to always be there, friends letting you know how much your friendship means to them, even if it's getting weird and creepy during the jukebox jam session. No matter who is important in your life, this song reminds us to tell them that they are. It's important, even if it is cheesy.

This is your soul tribe. Take some time to fill your heart with their love. It's cool.

PAGE

Are you so open to new ideas now that, when you look back, you see that you weren't ever as open to them as you thought? Does your new curiosity look nothing like what you have ever been interested in before, or feel like it ever has before?

Song to Help You Understand: "Up on Cripple Creek" — The Band

The love interest in this song is extremely unpredictable. She continues to be baffled yet completely enamored by her actions, such as tearing up gambling earnings for fun and listening to music she despises, because the message is cool. From the outside, it seems as if "Bessie's" fun-loving, yet erratic, nature is what's predictable about her. The singer is in love with the idea that he can rely on her consistently surprising him, so it's consistently an adventure.

New curiosity. Intriguing opportunity.

KNIGHT

Think of a time when your heart overrode your mind. Why did you let it? Did the thought of romance fill your heart with the idea that you had it?

Song to Help You Understand: "Insensitive" — Jan Arden

This Canadian crooner is asking a former love interest, over and over again, not just why he left her behind but *how*. How could he be so oblivious to her feelings about their time together? How could he have moved on so quickly, while she wallows in emotional purgatory? At a certain point in the song, her deepest fear about their history emerges, as she realizes her time with him might not even be enough to remember who she is. How could she have allowed herself to fall in love with someone who clearly never planned on reciprocating her effort? Perhaps the excitement of being with someone was more important to her at the time than who the someone was.

Heart-driven. Emotions over thoughts.

QUEEN

Who around you has that maternal vibe where, no matter what's going on, you always feel better after a visit with them? You know, that wise woman who always seems to know what you're feeling and always seems to know what's going on—and even what's going to happen?

Song to Help You Understand: "Someone" — Aaron Lewis

There is a comforting tone in the lead singer of Staind's voice as he pours his heart into this solo song. It's not just that this person is close to him, but it's the type of closeness that doesn't happen between many people, even in some romantic situations. It's not that the narrator's quirks can only be handled by who he's singing to, but that this special person can see much deeper into his soul, to the point where his actions can only be correctly identified by this "someone." Everyone else fails to see the real Aaron Lewis. It's not just that she tolerates him, but that she's cracked his code, and that is special beyond the words he's trying to say.

A special bond. A deeper love. An intuitive feeling.

KING

You know that person who it seems like they invented the phrase "turning lemons into lemonade" for? Who in your life always seems to have the situation under control, even if they themselves are on fire?

Song to Help You Understand: "Easy Street" — Soul Asylum

This song starts out with lead singer Dave Pirna relaying a rumor about someone talking a mutual friend off a high ledge, but the gossip is being relayed to the person whose heroism is the subject of the call. There is a bunch of chatter and elements to the story that no one is really clear on, but the important part of the story is that this hero was able to cut through all of the fat and save the suffering friend with a compassionate but straightforward approach. Despite the exaggerated drama surrounding the situation, this friend was able to make his way through the smoke and put out the fire.

In control of emotions. Gets the job done. Cannot be rattled.

A *Note from* Psychic Dee
(Orlando's Mom)

Hi everyone. This is Mom, and do I have a story to tell you!

I have been psychic since I was seven years old. By the time I was fourteen, I was already helping my teenage friends.

Before Brian was even born, we knew he would be special. When he was seven, he started to show signs. Picking up the phone before it rang and telling me who it was. Subtle things. As he got older, he denied the gift.

One morning, five years ago, Brian called me, and this is how it went: "Mom, how do I stop these dead people from talking to me? I can't concentrate. What do they want?" Needless to say, I was stunned. At forty-one, he was finally willing to accept his gift. I credit this to being around all the psychics at the radio station. My answer was—you don't deny it, you embrace it. He finally asked for my help.

I took Brian on the same journey that my mentor, Mary, took me on in 1972 when she saw my gift. We learned how to become spiritual, how to trust yourself when you "feel things" and how to be comforting to your clients. Be truthful, but caring.

Brian learned Tarot cards his way. Being in the music world, he decided to read by corresponding the cards to musical definitions. He found his niche. Now, he has the confidence to read dead people.

Brian has come a long way in believing in himself. He is caring and honest in his readings. Mom is very proud of him.

How Do I Read?

How do you read? You're the one holding the deck, so you tell me.

How many cards should I use? It depends on who you're reading, what you're feeling, and what you decide is *your* way of doing things. I have watched my mother spread out the entire deck of cards in the first fifteen minutes of a reading and carry on with profound intuitive messages for another forty-five. I tried reading with her once. After the first ninety seconds, I was begging for oxygen as I feebly tried to keep up.

How do *you* find that the messages come to you the strongest? Remember, the one rule that we teach at Rock'n Soul Tarot is not that there aren't any rules, but *the way you read in this world is within your rules.* You are the carrier of the messages. The cards are a tool. You are the one providing the intuitive wisdom. The cards probably cost around $19.99. If it only cost twenty bucks to determine the best way to decide on your career, love interests, future residence, and whether Uncle Sal will finally get over the Mets losing the 2015 World Series, the world would be boring, and life would be simple. The messages flow through *you.*

The first time I ever did a reading for anyone was just shy of a month after I came back from Mom's house in Tampa with her old Rider Waite Tarot Deck. I didn't have a fucking clue what any of the cards meant. Sure, I remembered their definitions, but to see them all scattered on a table resembling some sort of high school calculus equation, while the doe-eyed bartender from my local hangout, who agreed to be my guinea pig, stared back at me intently, was *horrifying*. What was I supposed to say to this girl?

I remember looking at a bunch of Swords cards upside down, the Kings of both Wands and Pentacles, and The Tower. There was no particular spread either. I just instinctively laid down three sets of three cards across the table. Panic ensued as I realized I didn't have a clue what I was doing. So I thought back to what my mother told me as she handed me the cards:" Brian, you really don't need these. Just remember that, and try to relax when you read someone."

So, I backed away from the anxiety assault and allowed my mind to open to feeling. To sound. To where the energy was leading me. My eyes kept darting to The Tower—that dreaded "it's burning to the ground" card that no one wants to see turn up. The people in that card who are falling from the window with the flames shooting out of it stood out to me. There was a reason I was fixated on *that* image. After another much-needed breath, Steve Miller's "Jet Airliner" seeped through the white noise in my brain, and I knew better than to dismiss the moment.

"If you don't spread your wings and fly now, you will never land at your next destination," I said steadily. More steadily, at least. It was probably the most stable my voice had been throughout the reading. Then I said it again. Then we started to talk, and my eyes started to lock in on different things on each card. Before I knew it, I was giving a pretty kick-ass Tarot card reading. Now, it was after the reading was over that my newfound favorite phrase—which I had never uttered a day in my life before that moment—was brought up: "You know, Orlando, right before I came here, one of my regulars offered me a job as a flight attendant on her private airline. Is that what you meant by 'spread your wings and fly' to get to your next destination?"

That's when the lightbulb went off. I mean, *of course* that's what I meant. See, when I did that reading, I didn't need a clue to do it. I needed my intuition and the trust in my guides to help me through it. Yes, you need to have trust in yourself, but I refuse to believe that this all just comes from me or you. It takes a village, and many of the residents have a much different zip code. This also provides a little buffer between your nerves and your conscience. It's not that you're cocky enough to think you can do this with little experience. It's that you're protected enough to believe your guides won't let you fall, or let down who's sitting before you.

Each week in class, I am asked very similar questions. In addition to "How many cards should I pull?" I'm frequently asked, "How long should I wait before pulling another card?" or "Should I let them answer first and then pull another card, or keep pulling while they're talking?" or "Do you hold the cards, or does the client?" or "How long should I shuffle?"

If you asked fifty psychics each of those questions, you would get over a hundred answers for each one. Every intuitive has a main method, and many have a few. The whole purpose of this book is to help you develop your *own* method.

What I will share is core to how I started my method. This is based on how my mother reads, with a bit of my natural personality mixed in. I always let whoever is receiving the reading shuffle. During this time, I ask whoever has the deck to think of what it is they would like to hear. If they're a compulsive shuffler, and it looks as if they're never going to be done mixing up the cards, I'll say something like, "Okay, I think you put a lot into those cards now. Let's see what the universe wants you to know." That usually breaks them from their shuffling trance, as no one wants to seem shallow arguing with some spiritual bullshit like that.

Like my mother, I then ask for the cards to be cut in three and then placed back into one pile in any order they see fit. Then I pull the first card. Now, I do recommend a small prayer before each reading. Mine is: "Dear Universe, please allow me the intuition, wisdom, and guidance to relay messages to my friend sitting before me to help them along on their journey and help them reach their highest vibration."

Once this is put out into the stratosphere, I'll study that card intuitively and look to it to set the tone for the reading. That card will sit above a nine-card pull. Then I'll have them pull nine cards from anywhere in the deck and lay them in three rows of three cards. The first row is the past, the second is the present, and the third is the future. Then, even though they can pick each card from a different place in the deck, I ask them to turn every card over the same exact way. If they flip the first card top to bottom for its reveal, I have them turn every card over that way.

I tell my students to let their intuition allow the cards to speak to them and not to worry if they can't remember if the Queen of Swords is the understanding one or not. She's going to be whatever she needs to be in the moment she appears, while surrounded by any combination of seventy-seven other cards. When you're reading, just ask her what she needs to tell you.

It's okay to be nervous. You'd be a real asshole if you weren't. We are talking about people's lives. Their emotions. Their secrets. To walk in all cocky and declare yourself "the gospel" would be a real dick move. Be patient and be honest with yourself and your reading, and be humble. The messages should soon flow.

A Note from Blair Flynn

I started working with Brian about two months ago. My friend bought me a 1:1 reading with him, and I was suddenly hooked. The reading wasn't at all what I expected, but it was exactly what I needed. I have been on my spiritual journey for quite some time, and while on this path, I've learned that this is typically how it goes.

Brian and I met in a coffee shop, and immediately he told me I gave him "cyborg vibes," to which I responded, "WTF?!" I have never been told that before, but once he explained his reasons for making such a conclusion about me, it totally made sense. I felt like I was a machine of a person, taking on some of the hardest things in my life at that point and constantly saying yes, even when I should have been saying no. The man knew me for 0.45 seconds, and he immediately knew what was going on with me.

Next came the part in which he communicated with my people on the other side. The first to come through was my friend Sarah, who passed away in March 2024. I wasn't quite sure that she would come through, given that we hadn't spoken the last couple of years prior to her passing, as she had given in to her former demons of drug addiction and lost the battle. We had lost touch in the last few years of her life due to her addiction. However, that didn't change the devastation I felt with her passing. I had, and still struggle with, some guilt of not being in contact with her. I think about her often. When Sarah came through in my reading with Brian, it gave me some peace.

One of the funniest moments in my reading was when I was trying to confirm it was her, and apparently, Brian had a message from her about not always approving of the men I dated. When I asked for clarification, he replied, "A guy who gave you a necklace." While I had a man in mind, that was too general a statement. When I asked for more clarity, Brian made a weird face and then replied, 'The fat guy with a small d*ck!" I immediately burst out laughing. While Brian surely didn't need to see that mental image, I knew that was my girl because she had no filter. That was her way of letting me know her energy was definitely in the room, and she wanted to get her point across.

I also lost my beloved fiancé, Bryan, in February 2024, and he came through in our session. (And yes, I am aware of the irony of the names.) He has given me some clarity on his passing and peace moving forward in my healing journey.

I have also recently joined Brian's weekly Rock 'n Soul Tarot group, and I have been hooked ever since. Again, while I have only known Brian for a short time, it has been an honor—and I am eternally grateful to have him as a new mentor, teacher, and friend on this crazy journey called life (and hopefully on the other side, if I'm lucky).

Imposter Syndrome

Every Wednesday, I host Rock'n Soul Tarot class at a local crystal shop in Sayville. We sit around a long table, with some lo-fi beats gently setting the background tone, and study three cards. I ask some questions similar to the ones you read in this book. Then we listen to a song that helps us further understand what we are studying about each card. Finally, we apply those lessons by coupling those cards with a random pull and applying what was learned to flesh out the story of a mini spread. These exercises not only help the students get a better feel for the card meanings themselves, but they also aid in developing their own spread interpretation and reading style. It's been fascinating to watch these students grow each week, while validating just a little bit more to myself that I am worthy enough to educate others on Tarot and their metaphysical gifts.

Today, as we hang out here together, I still worry about my worth both as an instructor and a reader. I question whether I have the experience and knowledge to be telling anyone about this stuff. Sometimes, a reading will go so well that I lose consciousness from the hugs I receive as the reading concludes. Whoever just shared their time and story with me will gush about how wonderful I was, listing all of the things I got right and affirming each name, date, and occurrence I picked up on. And yet, I *still* may drive home alone wondering if it was all a fluke. Maybe I just got lucky after noticing something they were wearing or recognizing them from somewhere, and neither of us realized it.

Does this sound nuts? Well...it is nuts. You wonder why anyone would want to put themselves through this on a daily basis. The truth is, I don't. But there are two reasons why you and I will, and do.

The first is that feeling of genuine purpose and love. You helped someone. You helped someone who may be hurting, and you helped them in a genuine way that cannot be measured by medicine or evaluation. The tears of hope, joy, and love. The brightening of a sad face. The look of relief on someone's face that you helped make happen will always overcome whatever fear and doubt you have. It's worth it every single time.

The other reason why the crippling sensation of imposter syndrome is necessary is that it keeps you humble. When someone sits down for a reading, their entire world is on display, as they appear before you metaphorically stark-naked. Sometimes, even the deepest secrets people keep locked inside get unchained and slip out. Problems that have haunted someone for decades can present solutions to the dilemma, which comes with serious emotional reactions. If we weren't humble about this work, it could be very dangerous. Imagine being such a pompous prick that nothing a client says registers with you because you have convinced yourself that whatever you feel is the gospel truth. Picture what could happen if you didn't present the heaviness of loss and betrayal or the horrors of assault with sympathy, kindness, and a gentle nature, and instead got high on simply being right, to the point where the person being read thinks you're enjoying their pain. That definitely wouldn't be right.

Growing up in this world, I have seen some of those types of readers, and it's not okay. If you're reading this and wondering what the big deal is about being like that with your gifts, you're most likely already a prick, and you should skip this part of the book.

Throughout the last couple of years, I have used fewer cards during readings and more of my connection to spirit, spirit guides, and the loved ones who come through to relay messages to loved ones. The word salad you just read is my gold-medal performance in mental gymnastics to avoid using the word *medium*. Heck, I'm only five foot six, but connecting to those who are no longer with us on this plane is the most common way I connect during one-on-one readings and hand everyone a card during a group setting.

I'll stand before a small roomful of those looking to connect with loved ones, or simply seeking spiritual guidance, and read the room while they hold on to whatever Tarot card was drawn upon entering. Before only the second time I ever did a gallery—as the professionals call it—my nerves were full of cannon-sized holes. I was a mess. *So the first one went well. So what? That doesn't mean this one will. I haven't been doing this long enough. These people are gonna think I'm a fucking fraud. Who the hell am I to charge people to see me? Fuck. Get me out of here!* Yeah, it wasn't my most rational of moments.

Everyone was sitting in a semicircle when I walked in. I convinced myself that these were all just regular people like me, and that their expectations were simply those of wanting a warm, peaceful night. I laughed. This is Long Island, after all. It's not like these people are traveling the world and running into psychics on every continent. Everyone is too busy paying these ridiculous taxes and just looking for a good night. I can do this. I can read the common folk because they are just like me.

I was ready. I sat on the table and scanned the room before me, noticing the working moms, the retired couples, the curious single women looking for guidance, Snake Sabo from Skid Row, an Italian woman holding a picture of ... wait, wait, wait, wait—WHO THE FUCK IS SITTING HERE? Common folk? The founding guitarist of one of my all-time favorite bands, who wrote some of my all-time favorite songs, *is not fucking common folk.* I'm about to do eighteen to life for smacking the stupid son of a bitch that told me this would be an easy night for regular people. Wait—I'm the stupid son of a bitch who said that.

After twenty years of radio, celebrities become a somewhat routine part of your life. It takes a minute, but you quickly find the balance of understanding how important their words are to your listeners. But if you talk to them like you would your best friend, they begin to sound like your best friend because they're more relaxed having a regular conversation. That helps you realize that many rock stars are just regular people who simply have cool jobs. That is how you handle interviewing and hosting celebrities.

Except this wasn't the radio, and nothing I learned in two decades about dealing with musicians I admire was coming to me. *Snake* was in the fucking room I was about to read. Snake!

I never actually settled down. I just started reading the room as if a gun was to my head, and this was how I convinced the person holding it not to pull the trigger. The first thing I said was "Timeshare. Timeshare. Aruba. Timeshare. Business decision. Who has the timeshare in Aruba, and you're facing a business decision about it?" Silence. Silence for *minutes*. Every time I asked the question, I scanned the room and saw only blank stares in return. Including from Snake. Five times I asked the question, and five times I was met with the same noise you'd expect from a cemetery at midnight. *I am a fraud.* I was about to fucking cry. The thing was, something deep down told me not to move on. There was a fucking reason I was stuck on this.

Finally, I locked in on a woman who seemed more interested in the floor pattern than my awesome *Top Gun* T-shirt. "Honey, do you have a timeshare in Aruba? What's the business decision about this thing?" This was at 8:11 p.m. The gallery started at 8:04 p.m. Snake Sabo from fucking Skid Row was watching. I was fucking drowning, but I now felt strongly that this woman with the posture problem could be where my energy was being drawn.

"Fine," she said with sheer exasperation. "My family has a timeshare in Aruba. We've had it for twenty-seven years." I asked why we rotated around the sun twice before she said something. "Because you said 'business decision.' We aren't making a business decision about it. As a matter of fact, we're actually giving it up next week. I don't want it anymore, so we're getting rid of it."

At that point, you would imagine rage would have taken over me, but it didn't. Relief did. *Maybe not everyone will be open to it,* I thought, *but I can do this.* The first ten minutes of that gallery kept me humble, while reminding me that connecting to spirit and helping others this way is a big part of my mission.

Toward the end of the night, a woman handed me the Tarot card I had given her as I first sat down. I couldn't even tell you what card it was, but it was from the Sun and Moon Tarot deck, and there was an image of a bottle on a beach staring at me. I took a breath and asked the card to talk to me, and two songs began to play in my head at the same time: the *Aladdin* theme and Christina Aguilera's "Genie in a Bottle." Yeah, it wasn't pleasant. But as I explained what I was hearing, we discovered that this was a message from a woman who was best friends with a person in the room seeking connection with me. Her name was associated with the lyrics of the songs, and she had passed over two-and-a-half decades ago. In all of that time, the woman attending my gallery sat before dozens of psychic mediums and had hundreds of Tarot card readings without finding the closure she desired with this fallen friend. Until now. It was powerful. It was emotional. It was deep. In fact, as I started singing a Lisa Lisa and the Cult Jam song, her tears spilled harder onto the tiles beneath her feet. The woman explained that her friend was a club girl, and that was the song she would be tortured with, as she preferred the heavy metal music of the era. "You know," she said, "like Megadeth and Skid Row."

The night wound up being magical, and that little lesson in the beginning was enough to remind me that, although we can make meaningful and powerful healing moments with people seeking our guidance, we are not gods. We are simply messengers. Not everyone will open the envelope and read what's inside, and that's okay. Be honest, be humble, and there will be no wasted time.

A Note from Melissa from Northport

At this point in our lives, we have all experienced various levels of trauma and heartache. Some old, some new, some new connected to old.

Orlando has productively utilized his role in radio to actively find creative ways to make us feel less alone. He often reminds us of the healing power that music can hold for us individually and when shared in a larger community. His voice has been a consistent and hopeful messenger that whatever comes up as we roll through life, music is the one reliable constant we can always connect with to help bring us through even our toughest moments and make our celebrations even more joyful and memorable.

Although we only connected on a personal level two years ago, in a somewhat magical way, we can instantly connect on a soulful level just by sharing stories from iconic moments from live music shows that we have both had the privilege of witnessing. It is one of the greatest blessings that we can remember experiencing some of the most brilliant and captivating artists of our generation.

I fully appreciate that Orlando makes time and creates connections in order for us all to have new music experiences to look forward to as we continue on our journey of life. Quite simply, he just helps us all to make our days a little sweeter.

What the Fuck is Wrong with People?

There will almost never be a time when someone sits down before you to get a reading because everything is awesome. What kind of raving psycho would look around while everything is firing on all cylinders, all their decisions seem to be the right ones, and everything they touch turns to gold, and say, "Man, I really need some intuitive advice right now"?

There is a very good chance that things suck for whoever is seeking your help, and if they don't suck, they're at least a little murky. They've come to you to help clear the smoke around the path in front of them. Therefore, your clients may not be in the right frame of mind to receive everything you're saying, at least not right away. Furthermore, they might not be ready to accept it.

We all have work to do on ourselves. If you're having a rough time, there is a good chance it's because you are refusing to make the necessary changes for a new beginning. So, if a Tarot card reader or psychic starts dropping some heavy truth on your lap while you're fragile, you may not be so open to hear what they have to say. That's not the psychic's fault. They're only here to give you the messages.

Now, picture yourself as the reader with that in mind. What you have to say might be exactly what someone needs to hear, but that doesn't guarantee they are ready to *hear* it, even if they are paying you for a reading. I've watched many normally rational adults get angry at my mother or me because they didn't hear what they wanted, which in their mind is what they paid for. So, how do you balance what you are supposed to say with what someone is willing to hear? Well, here are a few guidelines and even a few rules.

Do not predict death. EVER. If someone is bleeding from their jugular while standing on the edge of a mountain during a hurricane and asks you if they're going to die, the correct answer is, "That's not for me to say." We are not here to direct people on what road to go down. A true psychic is here to provide the best information possible to help you go down whatever road *you choose*. Free will is a main law of almost every belief system. I tell every client the same thing: "There is no future, only possibilities. The future is up to you."

I answer things like, "Am I in the right profession?" with "That's between you and your therapist." I feel for if there is a passion and then state what that passion is. Sometimes, it does not match the person's profession, and that can set up a series of questions that can help lead them to the answer they're looking for.

Be careful if you detect infidelity, but don't dance around it too long. Just ask. I would never look at the cards and say, "Ah, so your spouse is fucking around on you. Cool, let's pull another card." However, if there *is* a strong feeling burning through you, I would say something like, "There seems to be some serious trust issues in this relationship—do you suspect him/her of holding secrets from you?" If you suspect your client is the one being unfaithful, you can be a little bolder.

The first person I ever read for money insisted that I read her for money. Before her ass hit the chair, I had this feeling she was stepping out of her marriage, and that it was weighing her spirit down. However, I wasn't sure what I was doing and danced around the topic for about forty-five minutes before blurting out, "Who's this other guy with the muscles you're fucking?" This ... this is *not* the way to handle that situation. "Have we decided this marriage is over already?" would have been better. "What's the secret that's making it impossible for you to look him in the eye?" would have been better. These are people's lives. They're trusting you with these situations that shape their lives. It's an awesome responsibility, but it's a responsibility. Be straightforward. Be honest. But be gentle.

Other than that, you are basically left to call each reading as you see fit. Some may require tougher love than others, and some may need to be handled with kid gloves. There are some people who seem to have an infinite amount of money and psychic hope until they find one to tell them something close to what they want to hear. Some simply get offended when you nail it and immediately feel violated.

Around Thanksgiving a few years ago, I had a woman sit down during a fundraiser I was doing for a local food bank. She must have said "no" after every question I asked. It started to become a game. I would shorten the questions just to finish them before she could blurt out that nasty two-letter word. Over and over again, I kept hearing *no, no, no*. I was only doing fifteen-minute readings, so it wasn't going to be that bad. But as I looked at my phone and saw only eighty seconds had passed, I was about to bang my head against the wall.

Finally, I saw some legal circumstances surrounding a will. So I asked," What's with the concern over the will? Have we recently had some concern over a will and checked the details?" No. No. No concern. Finally, I placed my hand firmly on the table and stared straight at this woman. "Did you call your lawyer about a will recently?" I have never seen a woman look so angry—and I've been divorced twice. "Fine," she rolled her eyes. "I called my lawyer two weeks ago to check on the will, but I wasn't worried about it. I was just asking about it." Her next question, her *only* question after that, was, "Can I pay you more for a longer reading?"

It's easy to dismiss every difficult session as one with an "asshole" problem. But it's complicated. Some people aren't thinking straight. Some people need time to earn your trust. Some people actually are just assholes. That said, you can keep your cool by understanding that the person is there because they could be hurt, confused, misguided, or angry. It helps when you start to feel friction with a client. You are here to help them, but they have to want it. Tell them what you have been called to, and be there if they have any questions. And *rock on.*

A Note from Grace Grella

I first met Brian (in this lifetime, at least) as a guest on his Medium Ink with Jeffrey Wands *podcast. Jeffrey is the medium, and Brian is the ink, due to the massive tattoo collection on his body. (He is truly a work of art.)*

From the moment I was introduced to him, I knew how gifted he was as a medium himself, and thought the podcast should be called Medium Inked. *Brian was a reluctant intuitive at first, but I encouraged him and became a mentor for him to pursue his gifts.*

Music has always been a part of my mediumship in receiving songs and lyrics from spirits, and Brian, being a brilliant DJ and songwriter, was tuned into the same frequency. He would intuitively play songs on the radio for listeners that were relevant to loved ones, both in the physical and spirit world— creating healing through the music.

I am grateful for the connection with Brian, as I feel this isn't the only lifetime we have known each other, and I know he has a lot of love and healing to offer a world so desperately in need of his gifts.

How Do I Make Someone Believe?

You don't. You can't flip a switch on anyone, even after you've read them multiple times, picked up on their work issues, called out their deceased turtle from fifth grade's name, and saved them from an hour phone call with customer service because you accurately spelled out their forgotten bank account passcode. Some people will just turn around after all of that and call it a coincidence.

As I stated earlier, I grew up around Tarot and astrology and couldn't have a single problem without my mother asking the cards how to solve it—or looking to see what was in my fifth house on my second moon in Pluto to the third power to find out why things sucked. It was annoying and frustrating, and it turned me off to anything having to do with the metaphysical for the first four decades of my life. Even today, some questions annoy the living heck out of me.

"Am I in the right relationship?" I don't know, what does your partner think? "Should I change my major?" Depends on if you're gonna give the new one the same shitty effort you're giving this one. "How much longer am I gonna stay at this job?" Until you find a new one.

A few years into my run as morning show host at 94.3 The Shark, I was approached by a renowned psychic medium to do a show together on the air. Jeffrey Wands has been a staple of The Shark's sister station, Walk 97.5, for decades, and his show, "Psychic Sundays," draws people from all over the world listening online who sometimes wait on hold for hours for a chance to speak with him.

I would see Jeffrey around the station, but never as much as say hello, as my focus was on anything but conversing with the "weird guy who talked to dead people." One day in 2017, around the time my ex-wife and I were planning our wedding, she came to me with trembling hands to show me a selfie we took at Lake Ronkonkoma the night before. In the reflection of my sunglasses was an image that looked a LOT like her deceased father. So I responded with what any other cynical Italian who was sick of this stuff would say: "Baby, it was probably just the way the sun hit my lens." But my ex wouldn't let it go. "Could you talk to Jeffrey, please? He's on Walk tomorrow, it's the last Friday of the month." So, I made a promise that *if* I ran into him, I would show him the photo and get his opinion. I hadn't run into that guy once in four years, so I was comfortable with that vow.

The next day, I'm taking my usual 8 a.m. bathroom break, and who comes walking past me in the hallway? FUCK. Turns out that Psychic Medium Jeffrey Wands forgot the donuts that he gifts the building in his car, and he ran down to get them. So here I was, eating a Boston cream, making small talk with a guy who freaked me out with his annoying profession. Reluctantly, I pulled out my phone to show him the selfie my then-fiancé was eager to get his thoughts on. After a moment's blank stare, Jeffrey told me the name of the person reflecting back in my Maui Jim shades, his profession, and the way he passed away. It was my ex-wife's father, alright. He nailed it. *Probably just a coincidence,* I thought. *Maybe he saw a post I have never written on Facebook. I don't know.*

Later that morning, after he wrapped up his shift on Walk 97.5, Jeffrey appeared in my window. My hope was that he was simply offering me another donut and would then be on his way, but instead, he asked if I would be interested in doing a monthly show on The Shark, similar to the one he was currently doing next door. Now, I can be a stubborn fuck. Ask any of my ex-wives. But when it comes to radio, I am usually quick to capitalize on opportunities. *People love this shit,* I thought to myself. *This could be ratings, and it's not like he's gonna be reading me.* So, I told him, "Let's do it!"

After the madness of the wedding and preparing for winter promotions, Jeffrey and I agreed on the start date of December 8. That's a big date in rock music. One of my favorite guitarists— Dimebag Darrell—was tragically ripped away from us on December 8 in 2004, and if you go back even further, John Lennon was senselessly shot in New York City on the same date in 1980. Both of these icons are tattooed on my body. My tattoo artist Tommy is a huge Pantera fan, so tattooing Dimebag was a cool challenge for him. The Beatles, however, were the bane of his metalhead existence. I'll never forget him giving me shit the entire time he was digging his tattoo needle into my skin, as if I wasn't already in enough discomfort. "This is so fucking lame," he said. "If you love John Lennon so much, get him tattooed on your balls."

I hadn't thought about that since he tattooed me, and had no reason to. It was just another day with that wiseass. Now, here I was years later, listening to the tail end of Motley Crüe's cover of "Helter Skelter," while getting ready to introduce my new guest, when that forgotten conversation reared its head.

"That was Motley Crüe's cover of The Beatles' "Helter Skelter," as we ride into work together this morning on December 8th. Thirty-seven years ago today, we lost one of the main reasons we're all here, so we will honor John Lennon throughout the morning and showcase different bands he influenced. It's Orlando with you, riding shotgun. In just a few minutes, we will have Psychic Medium Jeffrey Wands on to hang out with us. If you're into it, hang out, and I'll give you the number to call to speak to him in a few minutes." And with that, I went to a commercial. Stoically, Jeffrey stared right at me. "John Lennon says thank you." I couldn't have rolled my eyes harder. Is this guy kidding me? Fool Long Island, don't fool me, bro. I looked straight back at him. "Oh yeah, Jeffrey? John Lennon's here? What else did he say?"

It was as if Jeffrey anticipated my doubt. With as close to a grin that the man could muster, he shot back, "He said thank you for not getting his face tattooed on your private parts."

By this point, the commercial break was over and the first song was just about ending. I turned on the mic and just froze. I had no idea what to say. *How the fuck did this guy know what my tattoo artist said to me five years ago?* I stammered so badly that I just hit play on the next song without ever forming a complete sentence. I did manage to pull it together long enough to get Jeffrey on with dozens of people. One after the other, he helped, he healed, and he provided hope as I sat there pouting and trying to come up with a logical way for him to have known so much.

When I got home that night, my ex-wife asked me how it went with Jeffrey. I simply said it was okay. I refused...*refused* to admit that he was dead-on with everyone, even the wacko that called in and asked if it would be her husband or her boyfriend to get her pregnant. I just wasn't gonna buy it. I saw it. I heard it. I just wasn't gonna believe it. For the next three years, one Friday a month and every Sunday, I watched Jeffrey and a slew of guests, including Tarot readers, astrologers, and an assortment of metaphysical experts, tell people things that there was no way they could have known, and I simply dismissed it all.

I wasn't ready. Some people may sit in front of you and think they're ready. Then the truth starts coming out, and the brick wall they suddenly run into stings so badly that they close off out of instinct. You know you're nailing it. They know you're nailing it. But fear, pride, and a combination of both won't let them *admit* that you're nailing it. So again, how do you get them to believe? You put your trust in the bond you have with your cards, in the bond you have with spirit, in yourself, and you believe in the message you're conveying. When they're ready to hear it, they will.

Look, your Tarot cards cost what, twenty bucks? Yeah, some decks have beautiful hardcover manuals or come within a limited edition series that drives up the cost due to their rarity, but what makes those cards valuable? They're special because they are *yours*. It's not the price. Not the scarcity. What makes them special is *who* they belong to. Sure, they could have been gifted to you by a loved one, and that makes them even more special, because then it's both about *who* they belong to and *who* they belonged to.

There is that long-standing belief that your first Tarot deck must be gifted to you. Personally, I think that's all a bunch of bullshit, because if you tell someone to buy you the deck, it's not exactly serendipitous, and if you drop incessant hints about yearning for a Tarot deck, people are just gonna think you're an asshole. If you bond with a deck, and that deck allows you to help people heal, focus, move forward, and maybe see things in a much clearer context, then who are you to say that it wasn't what the universe wanted?

There are quite a few of these traditions and superstitions. Some have been around for generations and date back hundreds of years. Did you ever wonder why some of these exist? I think it was in that show *True Blood* about vampires, where one of the humans didn't believe that another character was a vampire. The human said, "If you're really a vampire, then why can I see your reflection in the mirror?" or something like that. The vampire went on to explain that it was vampires themselves who started some of these rumors, so that it would be easier for them to blend in with humans and avoid getting a stake through their heart.

Now, I have zero evidence as to where and why some rumors about Tarot originated, but my suspicion is that there was a concern over who got their hands on the decks and what they would do with them if the intentions weren't pure. Remember, the people you are reading could have some serious issues that they are coming to you for. These issues could be rooted in realistic fears and wrongdoing, or they could be born straight out of paranoia, but there is a good chance that a person sitting before you at a reading is in a fragile state. A Tarot card reader not only has to be authentic but also responsible. I'm not exactly known as a subtle, gentle person, but you will never hear me say things like, "Oh, so your husband's been fucking your neighbor for a few years now, huh? When are you gonna leave that scumbag?"

There is a lot more to reading someone than having a strong command over your deck, and I feel the rumors like, *You can't buy your own deck,* were put in place to help control who is doing those readings. I also think the superstition of not buying your own deck could have some selfish elements to it. The more readers there are in the world, the less likely it is that someone comes to you. Professional psychics have been around forever, and I wonder if certain "traditions" were started to protect their practice as well as their practicing.

Another long-standing belief is that you can't use someone else's cards, like they're Thor's hammer or something. I've heard this many times, and even my own mother lets me use hers—and that's after a good ten minutes of hearing about how sacred her cards are, every time.

When I first began coming to terms with the idea of not only being psychic but admitting to it publicly, I was fucking terrified. I've endured multiple-hour tattoo sessions, been in bar fights, walked in front of moving vehicles because I was sick of standing at the red light in that rain, and every other stupid alpha male scenario you can imagine. Yeah, I've done all of those with zero hesitation. Seeking advice on what to do with Tarot cards? Fuck that. I was scared out of my mind.

I mentioned Lisa McGerity a few times by now. She's one of the most renowned Tarot readers and psychic mediums on Long Island. Lisa sells shamanic products all over the world and is now one of my most trusted friends. Back then, she was just someone a friend of mine introduced me to at her little Port Jefferson metaphysical shop, Envision Crystal. I mustered the courage to ask her if she could talk to me about what to do with my cards and how to do it, and she was gracious enough to invite me to the shop to talk one winter Saturday. I was expecting to hear all about what I should and shouldn't say, should and shouldn't do, and maybe even get some suggestions for tie-dye T-shirts. No, seriously, I had no idea what these people wore. I had no intention or expectation of actually *doing* anything.

The first thing she said to me while we were up in the loft of the shop where she usually does her readings was, "Okay, let's see if you're psychic. Pull a card and talk to me." She had such a sweet and soft demeanor, but she might as well have borrowed the growl of Satan's hungriest pit bull with that request as she sat there, holding out her cards while smiling like Greg to Mrs. Brady at the end of a "very special episode of *The Brady Bunch*." I wasn't ready. I wasn't prepared. I also had an out. "Oh, sorry, Lisa. My cards are in my car, and I parked up the hill." But she got around that one easily. "No problem," she replied. "Use mine. Here." Stammering, I began to repeat that old superstition about using someone else's cards and got shut right up. "Oh, stop," she said. "Come on, use these."

It's impossible to say no to Lisa. She's got this way about her where you just *know* she's right about things even if you don't want to admit it. So, I took a breath and drew a card. I don't remember exactly what was said, but she smiled, hugged me, and told me that she would help me. A few years later, she still is. Now, this is a woman who has a very strict creed. There are things she will always do and things she will never do, based on the shamanic side to her practice. When it came to me using her cards, she didn't even hesitate.

So look, no one can tell you what to believe, or even why. What I can tell you is that I have been lucky to know some incredibly disciplined protectors of the old guard, and they have instilled a fairly common-sense rules system in my head. I've also been learning as I go along that *you* will make rules as you go along. There are some pretty easy-to-understand guidelines, but ultimately, you make the rules. As long as your intentions are positive and you're not trying to hurt anyone, you should be good with whatever you decide is the right way to do Tarot. As long as you operate in the light, you're doing it the right way. Just don't be a dick.

Now *you* read. Read anyone willing to trust you with their circumstance. Marcy from the Port Jeff Salt Cave looked me in the eye five years ago and said, "I want you reading your cards daily. You need to do this. This is your soul mission." My first thought was, *Sure, lady, I'll break the stuffed animals out of the attic and see what's new in Teddy Ruxpin's life. Maybe 2XL is seeing a new AI chick.* (He's a toy robot who communicated through cassette tapes, if you were born after 1991.) Now, I don't have a death wish, so I explained to this very tough woman that I didn't have people around me who were receptive to this, so, no, I couldn't read every day. Now, she most likely smelled my bullshit from the moment I started talking, considering she knew my mother had been reading Tarot since 1966 and most of her friends were my "aunts." But Marcy simply replied, "Fine. Pull a card for *me*. Tonight."

Fuck. YOU? The student is not supposed to spar with his sensei on day one. However, I wasn't gonna argue.

So, I got home, I looked at a picture of Marcy from her website, and I pulled a card. Then I stared at that card. Then I stared some more. This was more nerve-wracking than any first shift for any radio station I had ever worked for. I remember how my eyes kept darting back and forth between her online pic and the card I drew for her. After a deep breath, I just started rage texting whatever flowed through my fingertips from my gut. Six digital pages full of stream-of-consciousness later, I hit send and waited.

When she responded, she did that annoying one-word-per-text for the first five texts thing.

BRIAN
OMG
WOW

Wow, what? OMG? Spit it out, honey, come on!
It went well. It went well enough that she called me and very emotionally encouraged me to keep going. So, every day, I reached out to a friend who I thought would appreciate a card pull and asked permission to read them. It just takes a simple, "Hey, can I pull a card for you?" Ask for a pic, if it helps you. I recommend it. Looking directly into someone's eyes, even

through your phone screen, can tell you a lot. Don't be afraid of the silliness that the messages that come to you come wrapped in. Just the other day, for example, the words "fuzzy wuzzy" poured out of my mouth like a bottle of teriyaki sauce with a broken cap. A grown, forty-something-year-old woman was watching me from across the table, saying *fuzzy wuzzy* as if my life depended on it. It turns out that *Fuzzy Wuzzy* was the nickname her friend in the pic I was holding had given to the stuffed animal she was gifted by the girl I was reading.

If you are blessed to receive something intimate, something sacred, chances are it won't make sense to you. It doesn't have to make sense to you. It has to make sense to the person you're reading. So even if it doesn't make sense, say it if you're feeling it. Many times, I have tried to put something off because it sounded ridiculous. But it just gets louder until you finally break. Just say it. When you're called to deliver a message, you can't fight it. It's not always gonna make sense to the person hearing it. That's okay, too. Something that a person hasn't thought of in twenty years might not come rushing back immediately.

In 2019, I was going through an awful time. Awful in the sense that July of that year looked nothing like March had. The pace was killing me, and the change was heavy. So I reached out to a highly touted psychic named Gina Simone, who had volunteered to help with some of my charity events for medically fragile children. She heard my state of mind in my voice on the phone and got me into her office the next day. Now, this woman is one of the most comforting and sweetest human beings on earth, but I was a nervous wreck. I hadn't had a reading since I was a teenager, and I was in my early forties, so I wasn't exactly clear-headed.

She opened the reading by asking me who owned "the white horse." No one in my family owned *any* horse. She kept saying, "It's a white horse in the family, and it was passed down." She wasn't letting it go either, despite the fact that I denied it vehemently. We finally moved on after a few minutes, and the reading turned out to be a much-needed, positive, and heart-warming experience—but the thing with the horse stuck with me.

Fast-forward a whole year...I'm sitting on my couch eating rice pudding in my underwear (Hey, I like to paint a picture. So did my great-grandfather, Pop Pop Tony.), and there on my wall, staring right at me, was his watercolor of a big white horse that was once my grandfather's before he passed it on to me. This thing had been on my wall forever, and yet I just couldn't place what this highly gifted woman was trying to tell me. If you and who you're reading hit a wall, ask them to write down the message so they can think about it at a later time. If you're feeling strongly about it, your message will show up to whoever needs to hear it when the time is right.

A few years later, that same scenario came back to me. A woman, who was very curious about her elder family members, sat down for a reading. She mentioned a grandfather who'd passed. I had some cards in front of me. At that moment, I got this image of a man in a fisherman's outfit, not far off from the New York Islanders logo of the early to mid '90s. Well, this looked nothing like the family member she was talking about. So, rather than stand my ground and look further into why I was seeing this, I moved on. Months later, she called me to describe the image I had laid out. It was in a painting that hung above this family member's chair on a wall in his dining room. The fisherman was a painting, just like my "white horse."

It's not always gonna make sense right away. Just keep going. Your intuition is stronger than you think.

A Note from Lisa McGerity

Every once in a while, you meet someone who feels familiar. Even if you have only known them for a short time, even just a couple of days, months, or years, it somehow feels like they have been part of your circle forever. This is my experience with Brian.

He wandered into my crystal shop one day with his best friend. The two of them seemed like unlikely crystal shoppers. They were just two guys hanging around in Port Jeff on a sunny Saturday. But Brian was seriously checking out the Tarot decks, and I could tell it was more than a passing curiosity.

Once we got to chatting, we compared notes on Italian moms and growing up around psychic experiences. His natural ability was hidden under a lot of fear and nerves. Brian isn't the kind of guy who wants to make a mistake or say something hurtful. Although, honestly, at times his delivery can be blunt. But I think that direct, funny approach is what endears him to his radio audience as well. Long Islanders tend to be a straightforward crowd. We all tell it like it is, and most of us are able to hear tough news when we are faced with it.

Tough on the outside, but soft-hearted on the inside—I've come to know a guy who started out tentative about this "spiritual stuff." He was unsure and curious when we first met. It seems like he was afraid of diving headfirst into the most woo-woo of the new age world. And, listen, I get that! I'm cautious and down-to-earth myself.

But, in the time I have known Orlando, I've seen his natural talent shine through. He's learned to speak the messages he receives. He's no longer biting his tongue and holding back.

He's using his gift now to help and heal so many. And isn't that just what the universe wants us all to do? I think so.

Communication is an art form. In my own work as a medium, I often say I'm just the telephone. I'm letting you know what I hear and making this conversation happen. Brian has spent an entire career in radio. He's a communication expert. He knows how to reach all his listeners across invisible airwaves and reach their hearts. He makes friends with people he has never even met in person. He's bridging the communication gap every morning.

No doubt, the radio work has prepared him for another amazing type of communication. He is using the same skill set to bridge the gap between the spirit world and our everyday folks. His easy-going style and casual way of speaking bring the Tarot to life and make the spirit world seem so close. It's a slightly different channel, but the invisible waves still carry messages—and he's the guy in the middle making it happen.

Having watched Brian grow and develop his skill set, I know we haven't even seen the beginning of what he can do. His new career will be amazing to watch. What I do know for certain is that he will continue making people laugh and touching hearts along the way. Keep your ear tuned to this psychic. He's got a lot more to say. Orlando is my new friend, who feels like an old friend. I'm sure we have known each other in at least a couple of lives.

Can I Read for Myself?

Sure. *Should* you read for yourself? I think that depends on what you depend on to make decisions that affect you and your family. Nine times out of ten, we tend to say *I should have gone with my gut* when things don't turn out the way you would have hoped. The thing is, though, are you being honest about what your gut actually said? Now that the situation has played out, were you *really* right all along, or is that just something you are allowing yourself to believe? At that point, it's almost like the consolation prize. "Wow, this sucks that everything just fell apart on me, but man I *knew* this was gonna happen. Next time, I'll listen to my instinct." If that makes you feel better, great. If that helps you make better decisions next time, cool—but was it accurate? Did you really know all along?

Here is another quick group of questions for determining if you should read for yourself. Are you able to accept news that you don't agree with? Are you prepared to make changes if the cards challenge you to make significant ones? Are you open to advice that contradicts your usual method of handling a situation?

I had a reading last year with a woman around fifteen years older than me. Now, I let myself go a bit, so I was positive she wasn't staring through me because I was being scouted as her next boy toy. She recognized me. She was my mother's Tarot card client since I was six years old. She even remembered the toys I would play with when she came by for a reading. So, we sat down, and I had her shuffle the cards. Her energy was very tense and vibrating out of her skin, so before she even drew her first card, I was ready to get started.

I stated a name and asked who it was, and why there was great confusion and depression. Her trance broke immediately, and as she shook herself back into our moment together, she explained that it was her niece who was struggling with her gender identity. Now, at that moment, messages started to fly, and as I watched this person turn over her cards, it all became clear what was going on—but then a funny thing happened. The woman I was reading stopped me. She wasn't there for her niece. She was sitting with me specifically to find out more about her son's health problems. She explained that the issue with her niece was one she was very concerned with, but her hands were tied when it came to helping her. Her son's health problems were becoming increasingly alarming, so she would rather I focused on him. Now, I have said this to many adults who sat in for a reading. I take requests during my day job. I'm here to read for you, not as a DJ—and I am not Burger King, so no, you cannot have this your way.

That doesn't mean I don't understand. You have something going on, and you're looking for guidance on how to handle it. It's just not always meant to be your problem to handle or solve. As I moved on with this reading, a relative who passed came up, her job came up, and many other situations that seemed important became topics the cards were showing me. But each time I tried to dive into any of these, I was redirected back to her son. So, I asked her a question she wasn't particularly keen on answering. "Why do you think we are hitting on every single aspect of your life but your son's health?"

Now, I don't call myself a psychic simply for fun and to write cool books on how to read Tarot, so I waited a few seconds before answering for her. "It's because your son doesn't *want* you to know about his health, and neither does the universe. This isn't your problem to deal with. This is for your son to face."

Yes, I realize what I had just done. Telling a mother to mind her own business isn't exactly the healthiest method for repeat business, let alone for making it through the current reading, but this was the reality of her situation. He wasn't telling her for his own reasons. Not mine. Not the cards. Not hers. The universe was clear to me on the rules of her reading, and I wasn't fighting a battle against its wishes.

So, this woman I just talked to you about—imagine *she* read her own cards. How many rounds of frantic shuffling would be done on her kitchen table after the last spread failed to show what she desperately wanted to see? How much would she huff and puff at the cards because their message didn't match what she was hoping it would?

I don't know if Jack Nicholson has ever had his cards read because, man, would I love to ask him if he can handle the truth. Can *you* handle the truth? Many times during readings, I have said some things that people weren't necessarily fond of hearing, but they accepted my honesty, even if they weren't accepting my words. That's the point of going to a psychic. You're looking for guidance. When someone else tells you something you don't want to hear, you have the choice to accept it or ignore it, but soon enough, you will be moving on. When it's just you and the cards, there is nothing stopping you from laying out new cards over and over until they resemble something you can contort into the advice you're looking for.

Tarot can be a phenomenal tool to help you through your day, month, year and beyond—but you have to be willing to accept not just its message, but its rules.

I have never done a reading of myself. Despite having more psychic friends than most women named Dionne, I may get read twice a year. I know myself enough to understand that I don't have the maturity to accept divine guidance on a daily basis. Some of my best moments came from my mistakes, because I learned from them. That's not to say you should *never* see a psychic, but read that statement with the same regard for one that reads *always* see a psychic. There is a proper balance of right and wrong, as well as what will and will never be in this world. If you believe that we all operate within a divine system, then believe that the universe isn't going to let you fall off the cliff as long as you don't play near the edge all day. When you're ready for intuitive guidance, seek it. Just know yourself, because no one else will understand you like *you* do—not even the best psychic out there. Advice is only as good as the person accepting it wants it to be, no matter who's giving it.

A Note from Katie from Huntington

I am a mom to three wonderful sons, and I built a blended family with my significant other (who will proudly tell you he's my better half) and his stunning daughter. I am an intuitive spiritual empath, deeply connected to music, crystals, Tarot, and the cleansing power of sage.

Now, as a Reiki practitioner, my greatest joy comes from helping others find light and clarity. Music is my constant companion—you'll always find me singing along, dancing, and dissecting lyrics for their deeper meaning. But enough about me. Let's talk about Brian.

I met Brian through Chris, an incredible intuitive energy worker and Reiki master. From the moment Brian and I spoke, we connected instantly. His voice felt familiar, and I quickly realized why. Brian is the morning DJ Orlando on 94.3 The Shark, the very voice that had accompanied me on my early morning commutes. We bonded over music, intuition, and Tarot, which he was just beginning to explore. (Looking back, I may have completely interrupted Chris and Brian's lunch that day, but it was clearly meant to be!)

Brian wanted to refine his Tarot skills and sought honest feedback. Without hesitation, I volunteered. When we met for a reading in the park, he uncovered things about my past that no one else knew. He saw my career dissatisfaction, my path toward finding my soulmate, and so much more. It was deeply emotional—I had chills. Beyond that, he recognized my own gifts as an empath and intuitive, understanding exactly what I was carrying and my desire to help others.

Over time, Brian would randomly message me with card pulls—always at the exact moment I needed guidance. A nudge, a confirmation, a sign to recalibrate. He just knows. Our connection is something truly special, and I'm so grateful to call him a friend.

Our shared love of music and helping others brought us together in ways I never could have expected. Even recently, I found myself unknowingly tuning into 94.3, hearing a song from my past that stirred up long-buried emotions, only to later receive tickets to "Story of a Song" and realize Brian was behind it. Absolute magic.

I cannot wait to read his book. If Brian has helped me this much on my journey, I have no doubt his words will inspire and guide so many others. I am grateful for his presence in my life and for the way he has helped guide me on my spiritual path.

Should I Feel Stupid If I Miss Something Obvious?

I was bullied horribly in elementary school. I was fat and poor. That led to a lot of ass-kickings and getting ganged up on. I was petrified to leave the house most of the time. I think I was around eight or nine years old when my mother had me talk with her best friend. My mother's friendship with Beverly was the kind that had me almost instinctively calling her "Aunt Bev" from day one. Beverly was one of those women who just had *it*. Tall, beautiful, and tough as nails. Even as a dumb little kid, I knew that she was special. Beverly saw how afraid I was of my own shadow and how shook up being in my own skin made me. She had me meet with her little brother once a week in an old garage to learn self-defense and martial arts. No, it wasn't called Brazilian jiu-jitsu back then. It was called, *This Is How You Deal With Assholes Class*. I met with Aunt Bev's brother for a few years, and the confidence I acquired, more than the fighting skills, helped make the bullying go away. My mother would read my instructor's cards as a thankful gesture.

Thirty years later, I met my buddy Teddy through the request line at 94.3 The Shark. I asked a trivia question about a rare supergroup, and he called in with the right answer. Jokingly, I accused him of Googling the answer, because I was the only one who knew the band existed, and he shot back that he was holding the CD as we spoke. From that day on, Teddy and I became like family, to the point that he was a groomsman at my wedding.

One of the early talks that truly bonded us was his confession that he was bullied as a child, and taking private martial arts lessons was what gave him the focus to turn his life around. My eyes lit up as I explained that I had an almost identical experience growing up. Despite Teddy having a decade on me age-wise, the universe seemed to hand us the exact same challenge to overcome. I raved about my mother's friend's brother and how he was a key factor in my becoming a man. How cool was it that two great friends were able to share that appreciation for martial arts in such a life-changing way?

Years had gone by between meeting Teddy and my finally embracing Tarot. I never really brought it up to him because it just didn't seem like something he would care about. I would do my Instagram lives and cite my rock and roll lyrics while holding cards on the screen, but anytime Teddy and I talked, it would be about what concerts we were gonna see or how badly the New York Rangers broke our fucking hearts again. So, it was just another morning behind the mic at 94.3 The Shark when my hotline rang at 6:07 a.m., just two minutes after my first break of the day. My eye rolls at that time of the morning are pretty severe, as it's just too early to be chastised about the lack of Iron Maiden before sunrise on an FM radio station. Except it wasn't an angry caller. It was my Aunt Bev. Twenty-five years after I last saw her. I was speechless. Absolutely speechless. My mother had been looking for her for two and a half decades, so how the fuck did she find me?

Well, it turns out that one of her Tarot-loving friends found one of my Instagram lives and told her to check me out. As soon as she logged on, she saw my face and immediately recognized me as her scared, chubby little nephew. So, she Googled me from upstate New York and found my profile page on 943TheShark.com. She and I talked on the phone up until the final second before I was live again. Once the on-air light turned on, I realized that I hadn't prepared a single thing to say, so I talked candidly about the sound of shock in my voice, how my beloved Aunt Beverly surprised me with a call, and how I had been talking to her this whole time so I was unprepared at the moment. I then explained how she once set me up with martial arts lessons with her little brother and how that alone was a big reason why I'm still here talking. It was a great radio break because it was honest, and anytime you have a chance to be human, it's appreciated by those who trust you to make their morning commutes suck a little less. One of those listeners that morning was Teddy.

By 11:15 a.m., I was in my car on the way home when my phone rang. What followed was hands down one of the dumbest conversations I have ever had outside of two in the morning bar talks next to a jukebox:

"What's up, Ted?"

"Yeah, so I heard you talking about my sister this morning?"

"Your sister? When?"

"When you were talking about your Aunt Beverly."

"Beverly Cain? Ted, what the fuck does this have to do with your sister."

"Brian, what's my last name?"

About five exits on the Long Island expressway passed me by before I was able to answer as I slowly, and I mean *slowly*, started to realize what Teddy did a few hours earlier.

"Wait... wait. Ted, *you're* the fucking guy who taught me how to fight?"

His response probably took another five exits, as he must have remembered how many times I spoke so highly of him, without realizing it was *him*, to his face. I remembered how many times he talked about how he knew he had to pay it forward after a man named Bob selflessly took time to teach Teddy martial arts. That story that blew me away with how similar it was to mine...it *was* mine! It was the precursor to what would become a crucial turning point in my life, to the point where I still talked about it whenever I could. What neither Teddy nor I realized for a decade was that I was talking about him. Teddy's wife, Caroline, still makes fun of us for being so dense, and we are in no position to defend ourselves.

Now, the big question. "If you're so psychic, how the fuck did you not know that your groomsman was your childhood karate instructor?" The question is annoying to any psychic who is faced with any sort of shocking incident. It's annoying, but it's worth bringing up here.

No matter how 'psychic' you are, you aren't designed to be reading all day, every day. We all have a million things going on in our lives, and even if your psychic antenna is always on high alert, there are everyday distractions that will numb any energy you may be feeling. Your sixth sense still has to compete with the other five that are rooted in the everyday mechanics of life's basic operations. Unless you're sitting down with someone who is opening themselves up for a reading, you shouldn't be feeling every single emotion they're going through.

In the case of Teddy's sister, they were pretty much estranged the entire time he and I knew each other. So, without her on his mind so much, her essence wouldn't just fly off his aura and into mine while we were standing at a bar watching a hockey game. This doesn't justify the two of us not putting two and two together, but chances are you are smarter than the two of us.

There will be obvious things you miss. It could be because you're being called to focus on other things. It could be that someone has closed off a part of their lives to the point where nothing is getting through. It could just be that you missed it. That's it. The cards got laid out, there was an obvious message in front of you, and you just didn't see it. No divine reason needed. We're human fucking beings. We get caught up in our own shit. It's another great reason to not go around reading random strangers as they walk down the produce aisle trying to choose the firmest watermelon for their June BBQ. Remember to give yourself a break, and everyone else, too.

When someone wants a reading, make sure the situation is correct, and do it. If *you* need a card pull, make sure you can accept what the cards say with an open mind. If something happens despite what you were feeling, or happened while you were least expecting it, deal with it and move on. There isn't a lot of time out there. Enjoy every moment you can. What didn't happen? We don't have that kind of time to waste thinking about it.

A Note from Janice Tverberg

As a psychic medium, I'm familiar with many of the tools used to communicate with those who have crossed over, including Tarot cards. Through the years, I've been drawn to and purchased several different decks of Tarot cards, but I've struggled to connect with them. I've found them to be confusing to understand, and they've never really made sense to me—so I gave up using them.

This has changed a bit since attending the Rock'n Soul Tarot class taught by Brian. I appreciate the way Brian approaches interpreting how the cards speak to us and their meanings. It's refreshing. He reminds us to throw away the book that comes with the cards and focus on what comes through to us from them. Why? Because the book will confuse the living shit out of you!

Relying on the book to give us the answers will most likely impede the real messages our clients need to receive. The meanings in the book will usually have little to do with the situation the person sitting in front of us is going through. Brian teaches that every Tarot card will have a unique and distinct meaning depending on the situation—and these meanings can and will often change if the same cards come up again in a later reading.

Brian teaches us to focus on what the cards are saying to us. What do we see, what do we hear, and how could this apply to the client sitting in front of us? This has helped me connect with Tarot cards a little better and incorporate them into my clients' readings when called to do so. Thank you, Brian, for being an unorthodox, fun, and insightful teacher.

Using the Rock'n Soul Tarot Method

Well, up until this moment, this very moment that you and I are sharing together right now, I never considered what I do as a "method" or a "formula." Makes me sound like, if you act right now, I'll send you a second book and a vacuum that will cut your hair. If you got that reference, I'm making a psychic prediction right now that you're dealing with some knee and hip pain and possibly get very angry when you have to bend down to tie those undone shoelaces.

The idea of this book, though, and the way I teach my in-person classes, isn't so much about you using my song choices and my life experiences to help you read cards, but to use the way I chose the songs and the memories to pick *your* songs and stories, and then develop your own collection of intuitive tools.

Let's practice right here, right now. We'll pick a few cards randomly and see if we can come up with songs and memories of your choice to apply to these cards.

The Eight of Pentacles—Leveling up. Reaching for the highest title, the furthest level possible for yourself.

What's something you're extremely good at that you have already taken to the next stage of its being, or at least are seriously thinking about? Are you a phenomenal cook that's told every time they serve meatballs that they should be on a restaurant menu? Were you a Boy Scout that stayed just to reach Eagle status? Are you in insanely great shape and are finally letting that desire to show it off on stage overcome the fear of the type of discipline and diet it would take to get there?

Now, I always hear Pantera's "A New Level" when I look at this card, but what do you hear when you read this description? Who faced this obstacle and achieved that next level of success? You? What songs were you listening to when you were working toward your goal? Think about your mom. What's her favorite song to get motivated? Someone you idolize? It's easy to look up their favorite songs and movies and who their idols are.

The Tower—This is a great card to practice with because we've all been there, and with radically different degrees of severity. If we have all been there, that means that pretty much every rock star, pop star, rapper, and definitely all of the country songwriters know what it's like when what you love isn't coming back. So let's look at songs that could help you understand someone's massive change through a disaster they couldn't prevent.

Divorce: "No Surprise" by Chris Daughtry. This song could have been written *in* The Tower while it was crumbling to the ground in flames. His lyrics agonize over what he is finally bringing himself to understand is inevitable. He hates it, he did everything he could to stop it, and he still doesn't want the relationship to end, but it's almost as if it's out of his hands. No form of reconciliation worked, and this couple has finally run out of excuses to start over, apart from each other.

Death: "See You on the Other Side" by Ozzy Osbourne. Ozzy has clearly come to terms with the loss of a loved one in this song, but he's still sad about it. Each verse serves as a cycle in his grieving. In the first verse, you hear him expressing his loneliness and the pain over needing someone who's no longer with him on this earth. By the second verse, he puts his faith *in* his faith and states his belief that goodbye is only temporary. By the third verse, he seems to have moved on and perhaps now is ready to take his journey to see this loved one again.

National Disasters: "Lightning Crashes" by Live. I was a teenager when the horrific Oklahoma City bombings happened. Hundreds lost their lives senselessly, and it was almost impossible to comprehend while navigating through the simple realities of high school life in the '90s. At fifteen on Long Island, I could barely understand why my teacher gave me homework, let alone why someone would kill hundreds of people to make some stupid statement. Then, a DJ remixed "Lightning Crashes" with news reports of the tragedy. I was standing outside my older friend's Buick with the T-tops off in front of my old house. The car radio was on, the engine was off, and we were draining the snot out of the battery. In an instant, whatever pseudo-adult drama we were clamoring about stopped.

I remember staring at that radio as if it were showing us the images on TV. The lyrics about the angels with their eyes closed and confused, the lines about glory hiding, and the natural elements of lighting, wind, and thunder that most of us associate with a bad day just ripped through me, as they interlaced with the shaky voices of reporters who spoke of death counts while sirens blared in the background. In an instant, I understood that the lives of those who knew the ones who perished would never be the same, that they were tragically altered that day. I wondered how they would love again, laugh again, feel human again. "Lightning Crashes" helped me understand one of America's biggest tragedies that day.

Music has a way of helping you understand. That's why using it to translate these cards that are speaking about people's lives is so helpful. If you decide to associate your own songs with these cards, take some time to study what happens when you listen to these songs. Who do you think of? What do you think of? What experiences, memories, and wacky thoughts come to mind that would help you translate what someone else might be going through if they were sitting across from you with the cards spread out? The beauty of it all is that it could be a different song that comes to you than the one you originally thought the card epitomized. Why? Use your intuition, the cards, and everything you have ever encountered, and find out.

A Note from Jonathon from Melville

I met Orlando through my girlfriend, Katie, who is an empath and spiritualist, often using sage to clear the room and always listening to music. This was after many struggles with an ex over our divorce and custody of my only precious daughter. I often wondered about loved ones who passed. Were they watching us, guiding me?

The first time I met Orlando was at a coffee shop. He was already seated, Tarot cards in hand, hat turned backward, as always. When he spoke—boom!—the voice. Unmistakable, the voice struck me first, over his words—a powerful, slightly raspy tone that reminded me a little bit of Joe Cocker, placing emphasis on certain words in a very musical way when speaking.

Strong in presence, tattoos marking his arms, he wasted no time and got right into it. He spoke of numbers that were relevant to me, loved ones, and the struggles weighing on me. He reassured me that things would be okay, and I would be okay, but he encouraged me to get into my spiritual self, too. The meeting stayed with me for weeks, and I had the opportunity to meet with him a few more times in casual settings.

If his book captures the essence of what we shared that day, I know it will leave a lasting and powerful impact on you. It is all intertwined and aligned with music, songs, and lyrics in a meaningful and yet inexplicable way. We each have our own story, our own lyrics, our own songs—they relate to us individually, and manifest and resonate in each of us uniquely, just as music does.

Should I Allow Readings to Be Taped?

I don't. I think it's a horrible idea. Think about what you might say in a reading. Think about how that might get taken out of context by someone with a vendetta. Let's say you uncover some infidelity. The last thing you need is a jilted lover running home with a tape of *you* talking about it. Just imagine ... "Oh, Harvey, do you hear this? Psychic Orlando said you were fucking Linda from Service. What kind of *service* are you getting from her, you son of a bitch?"

What you say to someone is in the moment. It's for them to use or ignore, but it's just for them. You don't want your words being taken to a friend so a third party can interpret what you said. Actually, let me rephrase that. They don't need your words being evaluated for their true, hidden meaning by anyone else. A one-on-one reading is a sacred session. And, let's face it, threesomes have a way of ruining the best of relationships.

That being said, spilling the details to your best friend the next day is almost always fun, so I do recommend taking notes. Take all the notes in the world, as long as it's not *your* voice telling the story. More times than not, you will say something that doesn't compute, and no matter how many different ways you try to word it, you're met with blank stares. Then, a few days later, you get a phone call. Your reading talked to a friend, and their friends reminded them of that time. Sometimes, your messages are for someone else in your reading's life. But I still recommend them being the ones to relay the message.

I did a Zoom reading with a gentleman in upstate New York once. He was cool as fuck and understood immediately why I didn't allow taping. I kept getting drawn to yellow roses once he mentioned his grandmother, and we discussed a story involving a bouquet of them that seemingly appeared when he went to visit his wife in the hospital. Each time his grandmother came up, the yellow roses on this particular card kept popping out at me. He had his notes. The next day, he called almost in tears. He had spoken to his mother about our session, and it turns out that his grandmother's wedding flowers were yellow roses, which were her favorite.

It was an awesome moment, and it was at that moment that I shared a story about my time working for a now-defunct classic rock station on Long Island. I was doing the afternoon drive shift and was asked to record a commercial (also known as a "spot," in radio language) for an "I Love the Oldies" party at the Shinnecock reservation. Well, it was 7:30 p.m., my shift had ended at 7 p.m., and I was ready to get the fuck out of there. My compromise was that I would voice the spot, but someone else had to produce it. Seemed fair to me. We had a production department for a reason. Well, when I walked in the next day, pumping through the house speakers in the main lobby—thanks to some carefully crafted editing—was *me* saying "I LOVE COCK I LOVE COCK I LOVE COCK" to a hypnotic techno beat underneath. It was at that moment that I vowed two things: Produce my own commercials *always*, and never let anyone tape you.

A Note from Bianca from Bethpage

I was a sophomore in college, not a freshman (more on that later). He was a dropout who owned a local club (it sucked and subsequently closed). We dated long-distance after I transferred schools.

On one of my trips to visit him...well, let's just say that after many years of therapy I can admit to having been date raped by someone I loved and trusted. Sadly, I stayed with him. Even worse, I soon found out I was pregnant. Then he joined the service, told me about it on the phone one night, and then I broke the news of the pregnancy.

His brother's girlfriend had an abortion a month earlier, so he didn't think it would be that big of a deal for me to do the same. I was going to school full-time, working full-time, and helping him care for a terminally ill family member. I had an abortion, went to work that evening, cried in the bathroom, and then studied for my math final.

Throughout the relationship, he would tell me that he had purchased an engagement ring, then returned it, then bought another one. It was not a healthy relationship, to say the least. One day, while he was stationed out west, he called me, clueless that it was my birthday, and somehow convinced me to visit. So, I went out there to visit and stayed for a few days. Things were looking up. But when I called to tell him I was back home from the airport, he refused to get on the phone.

This was about the time I first heard Alanis Morrisette's "You Oughta Know." I made a 120-minute (non) mixtape of that song. Over and over again.

After a few months, I started feeling stronger and more like myself. My painful past was in the rearview mirror—until I heard "The Freshmen" for the first time. Jesus, how I fell apart. Fuck him. The disdain I had for that song and the feelings that it brought back to the surface ... but the melody is haunting, and I do love it.

Fast-forward three decades...I called in and won tickets from Orlando to see The Verve Pipe at the Farmingdale, NY, studio. My stomach was churning. My husband couldn't get out of work (he's amazing, by the way), and I couldn't explain to anyone else why I would start crying whenever " The Freshmen" came on, so I never offered anyone else my extra ticket.

However, instead of making me sick, the show helped me heal an old wound. Listening to Brian Vander Ark (the lead singer of The Verve Pipe) talk about how the meaning of the song has changed for him over the years was cathartic for me. It allowed me to embrace the song in a new way. Plus, getting to watch Brian write on Orlando's hand with a Sharpie was the icing on the cake.

Orlando, thank you for the healing. Thank you for the memories. And thank you for letting me anchor that song onto a positive memory and a great day.

How Do I Handle Extreme Grief?

Well, that's really two separate questions.

Let's tackle the easy one first. *How do you handle your grief when you're doing a reading?* Listen, there are gonna be days when you get terrible news. Someone's ill. Someone passed. Your check engine light came on. So, how do you handle these things if you're scheduled for a few readings that day? The answer is *the best way you know how.*

I cannot tell you how to deal with your problems or determine how they might affect a reading. There might be a day when you're too upset to deal with other people. That's something you will deal with when the time comes. I know I have faced days where it didn't feel like I had the patience, the right attitude, or the strength to deal with someone else's issues. For me, though, almost always, once whoever I was scheduled to read sat down and started cutting the deck, anything that was bothering me quickly dissipated. That's not to say reading someone made it all go away, but once you learn to lock into a reading, there is a good chance that's all you focus on. Like any high-level professional, you leave your baggage at the door and get the job done. Only *you* can determine what parameters need to be set and what *your* mindset needs to be before you read.

I will say this, though. You hear it all the time in this world: "The Universe sends you people, and each reading was meant to be." That might be the case, but no one needs their time wasted hearing about it. I'll give you an example of what I mean. You may have just found out a few minutes before a reading that your pet passed away. That's always gonna suck, but somehow you decide to power through, because whoever asked you to read them needs guidance more than you need a hug. If you feel up to it, you go through with it. Cool. Now, you discover five minutes into the session that the person you're reading just lost *their* beloved pet. You might get the urge to immediately interrupt with, "Oh my god, my dog just died ten minutes ago. I was meant to read you today! The Universe wanted us to connect." Don't do that. They're paying you, or at least trusting you, with their time. After the reading, you can tell them that you understand their pain and explain why. *During* the reading is their time.

I have seen quite a few students come and go during the year or so I've been teaching Tarot publicly. Some started at week one and haven't missed a class. Some stop in every once in a while for some laughs and camaraderie. Some hear the amount of F-bombs that I drop and run to the church a block up the road. Only once did I make sure a student didn't come back. She was an intermediate reader, and I always try to appreciate anyone who feels my guidance using Tarot is worth their time. From the beginning, however, there was just something about her that didn't sit right with me. But again, she was in my class to learn, and that's cool. It wasn't like I was looking to date her.

After a few classes, I noticed myself more and more agitated each time she spoke. I tend to get lost in teaching class, as I'm constantly holding up cards, playing songs, and going off on tangents, so it took me a bit to realize that she had something to say after each example I gave. No matter what card we were learning, she had a personal story that she needed to share. The Two of Swords? Forget about my lesson, she had a major decision she's still feeling. Just stop and listen. Temperance? She's so busy. Drop everything and hear about everything she juggles. Your typical one-upper. You got a ticket on the way to class? She got three. You spilled your coffee on your shirt? Someone dumped the pot on her.

This is not the vibe you want to give as a reader. It's not about you. It's about them. That's something we should all always remember, even if you are well intentioned in sharing your story. There is a time and a place, and although that one student never understood that, you and I can—and it makes you a much better person to get a reading from.

Now comes the second question: *How do you read someone who just suffered a devastating experience?*

Probably the same way you would talk to a friend who is coming to you for a shoulder to lean on. If you tend to read quickly, slow down. If you're someone who just blurts things out at a rapid-fire pace, a lot of what you say might get lost on someone struggling to keep focused enough to hold back their tears. We touched on recording sessions in a previous chapter, but even if you do allow taping, have someone who isn't extremely distraught write down what you say. Many times, they aren't thinking about what you're saying at that moment, so once you establish a rhythm and things start to flow, you can revisit the list of things you moved on from and see if it makes more sense once they're calmer and you've built trust.

No one comes to you when things are great. We also carry a lot of baggage—*all* of us. If you don't, fantastic. I'm happy nothing ever went wrong in your life. But for everyone else, they might have a few traumas coming back up from time to time. You are trying to break patterns so the person doesn't keep hitting the same dead ends. A reading is someone's past and present, and the possibilities ahead. So, be prepared for some of the most uncomfortable situations to come up. Unexpected death. Drug addiction. Domestic violence. Sexual assault.

You may be shocked by how open people are with this stuff. Sometimes, it's easier to talk to someone you don't know, and the loophole is that, as a psychic, you are establishing a level of trust using validations as if you *do* know them. So, don't be shocked when people lay it all out on the line. Be respectful but honest. The second you hear something out of their mouths that crosses a line, decide right then and there if the reading should continue. Most times, it's just people trusting you with extreme pain. You can always refer to what Peter Parker learned about responsibility as Spider-Man: You don't mess with people's lives, and you can't stop people from messing up their own. Just be straightforward, honest, comforting, and ready to receive what they need to be told.

A Note from Jamie Lynn

Once upon a time, I had a job I commuted to daily, right down the road from the headquarters of 94.3 The Shark. Every morning, I would tune in to this "new" DJ who seemed to have a similar affinity for my favorite '90s alternative rock—and the kind of natural delivery that made inching along through Long Island's rush-hour traffic infinitely more tolerable.

Fast-forward more than a decade...while the job and the commute may be distant memories, the DJ remains. Toss in a couple of serendipitous happenings and the timing of the universe, and I'm grateful to say that the voice became a person, and that person became someone who has gone out of his way to help me over the course of the last year, on both a personal and professional level.

But it all began with the music, as most of life's best things do.

Everybody's Friend

There have been some moments in my radio career that have gotten more than a little annoying. Being in someone's car every day, sharing personal stories while they deal with the bumper-to-bumper, rush-hour commute, becomes a very personal thing. For every spilled coffee on someone's lap while rushing to not be late for the fifth time in four days, for every middle finger given or received while changing lanes too closely, for every fight with the significant other on speaker phone...I'm always in the car with them. At least my voice is. It can be very easy for someone to forget that I haven't met them in person.

There have been countless times when listeners have sat down at my table, as if they'd walked into the restaurant with me, and just started answering a question I asked on the air three days prior. There have been countless stops at traffic lights, when a voice from the car next to me screams, "Orlando, play more Maiden!" (Seriously, it's always Iron Maiden.) And, thank god for earbuds, because it was really annoying when people would pull my headphones off my ears in the middle of my workout to tell me how cool it was that we go to the same gym. Yes, I want to punch these people, sometimes, especially when they somehow get a hold of my personal number and text me random questions about who Metallica's official first guitarist was. It's invasive. It's intrusive. It's rage-inducing. That said, it's a major sign that you are very good at your job.

The whole point of someone turning you on every morning to hear your thoughts, as the person listening struggles to get through their daily grind without a felony charge, is to feel familiar. A morning show host is someone's lifeline. Someone's friend. Long before I ever got behind the microphone, I sat behind the wheel of a twenty-six-foot refrigerated box truck with a tight schedule in front of me. Those Long Island DJs got me through the worst of it. It's funny, my direct competition for the last decade, Roger and JP, were a major reason why I survived my routes most mornings. They were, and still are, a first-class production and great jocks, because they understand just how important it is for someone to have a reliable, relatable voice in the morning.

Being a good psychic carries an extremely similar responsibility. People are coming to you hurt from a fight the night before, worried about how they're gonna pay the bills this month, anxious about an upcoming surgery, and just looking to survive the day. You're getting a week's worth of commuters' thoughts in one sitting. The entire process works better if the person you're reading feels your friendly energy and your warmth. If you met me, "warm" wouldn't be the first word you'd pick to describe me, but I've been told my honesty is comforting. That's all people want. That's not to say they can handle it or accept it, but the truth is a comfort—and you are being met with to provide that comfort.

In time, you will get to know someone better than most of their trusted companions. You will know their deep secrets and embarrassing confessions. You will become their spiritual friend. Now, we have talked about boundaries, and common sense doesn't need to be mentioned here, but keep in mind that the topics of conversation you are sharing are sacred. It's impossible for someone to not feel close to you. Understanding that has helped me steer clear of some extremely awkward situations in both my radio career and in the spiritual guidance world.

Back in 2015, a publicist had reached out to me about some last minute promotion for the band Sponge, which was coming into town in a few days for a show. If there was a word faster than yes, I would have shouted it. SPONGE? As in "Plowed"? "Say a Prayer for Me"? You mean Sponge, the band that does

"Molly (16 Candles Down the Drain)"? That *Rotting Piñata* CD had been with me for some milestones of teenage dirtbaggery. That band had been playing during some of my most epic moments, and hell, some of my most shameful as well. That band had been with me since I was sixteen.

I believe the publicist's name was Dana, and the two of us set up a radio contest where 94.3 The Shark would give away a backstage meet-and-greet experience, including dinner with the band. The pre-arranged phone interview with Sponge's lead singer Vinnie Dombroski to promote this pretty cool band experience was a riot. I had never met Vinnie in person, but our scheduled twenty minutes turned into about an hour and a half of laughing, sharing music choices, and getting some behind-the-scenes insight as to what being in a band during the '90s pop culture revolution was truly all about.

The night we met in person was as easy as the phone call. Here was a guy I had just spoken to once on the phone, having a full-blown conversation with my girlfriend at the time about whether vaccines cause autism and how the media makes so many problems in the world. You know, those taboo topics you don't bring up at dinner? Yeah, we shared thoughts about all kinds of things without worrying about who was gonna get offended. From that point on, Vinnie became one of my most trusted friends in radio. He has donated countless hours to charity events, musical projects, and other wacky ideas I've had over the course of ten years. He's someone who taught me how to handle the line between people who know you and people who *think* they know you. Even though Vinnie and I hit it off instantaneously in 2015, it wasn't until 2018 when I asked him to participate in a musical endeavor for suicide prevention. It was after many talks about depression and mental health that I felt comfortable enlisting his help to sing on a song I wrote, even though he felt like someone I could have asked on the first day.

When you become a professional reader, you should be someone a stranger feels comfortable talking to. Yes, it gets really weird, but just like in radio, and just like in rock and roll, it's part of the job. You are the voice people need at the moment, and that voice is much easier to accept if it sounds like an old friend talking.

A Note from Margherita from Merrick

On behalf of my late husband, Dan, I have to speak on Brian's connection with him. Dan has been a fan of The Shark since day one. He really connected to the way Brian spoke about music, his knowledge, his passion. Music was Dan's way of connecting to the world. He was a quiet guy, but when he started talking about music or sports, that was where he really opened up and flourished. I used to joke that he could definitely be a rock DJ with his knowledge base.

For years, Dan reached out to Brian through the radio station or Facebook, and the two slowly but surely started forming a connection. He would attend Brian's birthday bashes every year and support a lot of events that the station would host. From there, they built a beautiful friendship.

Brian was there for Dan during some personal struggles. He respected his insight. When my husband got sick, Brian really showed him how much he appreciated their relationship. That meant the world to Dan. The fact that Brian was there at his wake, along with the shout-outs that he's done for Dan, means everything to me.

Brian, you are a special person for what you've done for my children and me. It will always be remembered and appreciated. You absolutely rock, pun intended. Thank you for being you.

Are You a Psychic or a Therapist?

This is where it gets tricky, because you *will* wind up with people who rely on you. I don't recommend you get involved in anyone's life. Many who sit before you will find some peace and experience some healing, but that doesn't mean they no longer need professional therapy. There are amazing holistic therapists out there who speak the same language we do, and might even understand a piece of advice they're bringing to them from you. However, it should never be our job to substitute anything. We supplement. We guide. We help. We don't replace. There are people who run to me the second something goes wrong. I've had people knock on my door at all hours of the day looking for my mother in a frenzy because they just got fired, or ring the house fifteen times in a two-hour span due to their decades-long marriage suddenly falling apart.

I understand *why* someone would seek you out first. A great reading not only provides valuable insight, but also soothing energy that may be lacking in other areas of your life. It can be addicting to have someone "get" you if you're not being understood anywhere else. That doesn't mean a psychic should be the first person we all run to when the shit hits the fan. There are reasons we don't know everything. Sometimes we're meant to head down certain roads, and we need to be a little lost to stumble upon them. Having all the answers now might mean missing something later, based on how it shapes your decision-making. I know that's just a fancy way of saying, *sometimes we need to stay in the dark a little longer because the light burns.* If

164 | Brian Orlando

you want to steal that lyric for the next great American rock single, go for it—but there are rules for a reason.

I can't remember if we mentioned it already, but I have a No Readings Within a Three-Month Span rule. Life has to have its room to play out. My mother's rule is every six months, but I feel that many people I read live in a much faster-paced world. Mom is seventy-three. If you're reading this in its first year of print, I am twenty-nine (wink, wink). If you are gracious enough to pick up the fifteenth anniversary edition one day, I will still be twenty-nine.

Now, I mentioned therapy for a reason. I believe in it the same way I believe in psychic readings. Therapy is a very important and necessary tool...*if* you put in the work. You're just burning through a co-pay if you sit in front of a professional for forty-five minutes, only to dismiss every single thing they said to you.

Right around the time of my second marriage falling apart in 2019, my life was following suit. Not only did I reach out to a psychic for the first time in years, but I found a therapist. I was forty-one. My last session with a mental health professional before that was when I was twenty-three.

Tracey Cardello is a holistic LCSW, which took me about two years to memorize as licensed clinical social worker. I noticed a few things while scoping out her website looking for someone to talk to about my life crumbling... yet again. Tracey's approach focused on root causes of core issues. She believed in a mind, body, and soul connection that focused on both the conscious and unconscious. She empowered you and taught muscle testing and EFT (Emotional Freedom Technique) tapping. I thought to myself, *Wow...what a crock of utter bullshit this is.* And then I called her. Why? She looked super attractive in her pic. Look, I never said I was smart or sophisticated.

The funny thing was, it was around this time that I slowly started to feel my metaphysical path creep up on me. Tracey's sessions reminded me of a reading with my mom. I felt Psychic Dee's clients' same sense of rejuvenation and hope each time I left Tracey's office. I felt that there were choices and they were mine to make, and having a little clarity as to why I kept making bad ones gave me a newfound confidence to make better ones moving forward. I truly believe that my sessions with this extremely talented psychotherapist and healer allowed me to understand why people sought out my mother—and, soon enough, to see the bigger picture as to why they would sit with me.

By March of 2020, the world had shut down, and we were all in desperate need of some guidance. Tracey volunteered her time every single week to offer advice and messages of healing during my morning-drive radio show. She was an invaluable tool for those who struggled to make sense of perhaps the most bizarre time in any of our lives. It's something to think about when someone calls you frantically for your services. Think about how we all felt as our lives suddenly and painfully changed. How out of control we felt. How different the world looked all of a sudden.

When someone is seeking help, whether from a reading, a psychic medium session, a visit with a mental health professional, or a visit with that one friend who actually fucking listens, their world looks drastically different. It looks foreign. It looks impossible to find your way in. That's why someone is coming to see you. I admit, I wasn't completely open to Tracey's methods when I sought her professional help. Someone might be too broken to suddenly hear about all of the changes the cards are telling them to make. It takes patience, peace of mind, and practice. Be mindful, be respectful, set boundaries, and be firm on your rules.

A Note from Doreen Farber

Many years ago, while listening to my favorite genre of music on the radio, a voice popped up after the song that felt like a familiar friend. I felt like I was listening to someone I knew at the bar after a long work week, needing to unwind and rant.

When I'd have a particularly bad day, it would always feel like having a hot cup of coffee on a rainy day to turn the radio on and listen to Orlando talk about all the odds and ends of life. It also didn't hurt that I learned a lot about the songs I grew up with but never knew the meaning behind. He was always a token of wisdom and a familiarity we can relate to on a deeper level, and I think, inevitably, that's what this great thing we call music does to all of us. We learn to relate to each other through it.

Orlando has shown me that, at the end of the day, we are all a little bit connected to each other, and that music touches humans more than anything else.

How Do I Approach Others About Readings?

You don't. If you want to be taken seriously, you don't use that as an icebreaker. On multiple occasions, I've been asked to be a part of fundraisers that use psychic readings to raise money for various charities. That's the easy part. Helping others? Helping animals? Let's rock. Listening to other people brag about themselves? Ugh. Usually, these events consist of a few different types of psychics and readers, and it requires at least one organized meeting to get everybody on the same page.

I will never forget this one, quite ragged-looking woman walking up to me as if she were about to ask for change for a coffee. "Hi," she said. "What do you do? I'm a medium. I also read aura." Now, I didn't leave her name out for protection. She never said it. Her icebreaker was essentially: *These are my superpowers. What are yours?*

Now look, the work we can do is special, but by no means should it be used to make *you* special. You're special because you're you—not because you have an extremely accurate take on the Ten of Swords as it sits menacingly next to the King of Pentacles. We're here to help those who find us. I am not against advertising, as a whole. The Universe isn't gonna do all the work for us. You want to post stories on Instagram, do Lives, make cheesy commercials that would make Miss Cleo cringe—go for it. People can skip them or turn them off. What they can't escape from is you shoving what you do down their throat.

If someone asks what I do, I will tell them. If they have further questions, I will answer them. What I will never do is ask someone if they want a reading. To me, that's the sacred line. If you have a friend in need, pouring their heart out to you, listen to them and then offer advice. *Your* advice, not the cards. If they ask you to pull a few cards, then do it, but remember that *you* have a lot to offer people too. All too often, I have seen psychics rush straight to their decks to respond to anything you ask them. It's off-putting to anyone who just needs someone to talk to. It also devalues yourself as a trusted confidante. If all anyone wants from you is divine guidance when they talk to you, they're the metaphysical version of what in radio we call a "prize pig."

A prize pig is an on-air DJ's biggest pain in the ass. Your job every day is to be as entertaining as humanly possible. Prize pigs live for appearances to get their ninth free T-shirt. They flood the hotline to win yet another trip to a tropical island. They use multiple phones to get that final pair of tickets to a show many others haven't seen yet. At times, the can be entitled, arrogant, and flat-out boring. Thanks to budget cuts, poor management, and sometimes just utter stupidity, that's becoming an increasingly difficult task. Even most morning shows have become one-man operations. Airing phone calls is the one opportunity to offer your listeners another voice, someone else's opinion on a topic.

Prize pigs aren't interested in conversations with you. They want their tickets, and they want to hang up as quickly as possible because the next station on the dial has something they want, too. Appreciation is almost never expressed, and that makes for an infuriating experience to anyone who couldn't get through who truly wanted what we were giving away. Imagine driving through bumper-to-bumper rush hour traffic, missing out yet again on something cool that would make the day a little better, and hearing the *same* unappreciative, entitled voice rushing off the phone without so much as a thank you.

Yeah, this is radio pretty much 24/7. These same people walk up to jocks at events without so much as a hello. Their icebreaker is usually, "What are you giving away today?" or "What, no T-shirts in my size?" If you think I'm exaggerating, call your local DJ tonight and ask them. When I hear someone lead with, "Hi, I'm a psychic," my instinct is to hang up on them and wait for HR to read their complaint email to me.

Not everyone has the time for this stuff. Not everyone trusts it, and it's only your job to prove the importance of it to them once they actually sit for a reading. It's not your job to persuade them to sit. Once you become obnoxious about it, you might as well buy two more phone lines and wait for me to ask for caller nine. I'd think you're a dick for that, too.

A Note from Brian Dalton

When Rock 'n Soul Tarot came up on Spotify as a recommended podcast, I had to listen. At first, it was because I wanted to know more about the meanings of the cards. I soon found myself coming back to Brian's stories, histories, and explanations of songs. A lot of the performers Brian talked about are people I am a big fan of, especially some of those bands from the '80s and '90s. Tarot became a secondary reason to listen.

I have a lot of respect and admiration for Brian because I see what could have been for me if things happened differently. Growing up, music was a huge part of my life. As a junior in high school, I had two classes in our music room. As a senior, I was there for half of my day. That's not counting the time I would spend on rainy days and literally every day at lunch. The music room was my home away from home. I never got good at guitar, but my time there and the people I spent time with are probably why I am still here on earth today. During that time, I seriously considered becoming a music producer or radio DJ after high school.

When I listen to what Brian has to say, I feel like I'm back in Mr Kupka's music room, where we unofficially started sixth period with one of the students playing "Paranoid" by Black Sabbath on his guitar. I've embraced a love for cooking in the past decade or so, because music, just like food, is one of the few things in the world that brings people together regardless of their differences. Brian's content is a reminder of that. The way he talks about music inspired and excited me in a way that I haven't felt in a long time.

How Often Should I Read People?

Depends on who you're reading, as much as how many people you're reading. If you're dealing with three people, and the worst of their problems is that the husband can't stop buying sports cars or someone's grandfather refuses to stop calling his grandkid chubby, then those are probably three readings that won't require much aftercare. If you have three readings back to back to back, where you're dealing with suicides, betrayal, and rage...you may need a few moments before you dive back in.

Now, the question is probably obvious: "Well, how the fuck do I know what kind of readings I'm gonna have?" Yeah, I mean, I don't think any of us are *that* psychic. Sure, I have felt accidents before a reading. I have felt death before a reading, so you *know* it's gonna be heavy. But depending on how someone processes things, you can be laughing your ass off through the entire experience. Just one memory of a loved one, even one who passed horrifically, can spark the biggest moment of joy, and you will walk out of that reading as elated as who sat before you.

Then you can have days when everyone is an asshole. The "I'm gonna sit here and you're gonna impress me crowd," and they're not gonna give you anything if you're off by a single letter. They can leave you utterly exhausted after forty-five minutes, to the point where you don't want to talk to the drive-through clerk for dinner, let alone do another reading.

I was reading at a party once. There was one other psychic there with me, and the crowd was a decent size, so I was looking at about fifteen to twenty people to read. About midway through, a heavyset woman sat down. (Yeah, I don't know if *heavyset* is the right term now. I can't keep up.) Anyway, as the reading started, I said, "What's the living situation with Marie that's no more? Why are we going backward with that? Living situation with Marie?"

This woman defiantly shook her head no, and did so repeatedly. Yet I felt strongly about this, so after several attempts to vary the question failed, I asked her the name of her college roommate who she'd just rekindled a friendship with. "Oh...Maria." Trying not to flip the table over, I said, "She's the one who gave you a hard time about your weight?" She replied, "Oh my god, yeah. How did you know I had problems with my weight?"

Now, even though I had an estimated eight to ten people left to read, I took a ten-minute recess to reset. You can't always dictate the terms before a reading. Sometimes, you won't have time to meditate or decompress or whatever, but when you can, you should.

If you're just starting out, I would limit it to one full reading a day. This will give you an opportunity to gauge how much time it takes to feel like *you* again, if you need it at all. Good for you if you don't—but you will. Another great way to build your endurance is to volunteer for some charity psychic nights. Usually, these are set up in a way where a person sits before you every ten minutes or so, and you can get up between each one for a water or bathroom break. Even if you just need air, you can dictate the pace. As you get through a couple of these types of events, you will quickly get an idea of what kind of space you need, depending on how the reading goes. And when you're reading five to ten people to start, chances are you will experience a good sample size of every type of psychic scenario possible.

My radio shift is over at 11 a.m. When I started at 94.3 The Shark as their full-time morning show host, I was thirty-six and looking for nothing more than to talk and hang out. I'd go from my on-air shift to the production studio for an hour or two, and then straight to a local bar for lunch and a drink. Within minutes, I would be bombarded with questions like," What happened with that one caller you hung up on today for cursing?" or "Why do you only play thirty-two Bush songs, bro? They have so much more."

It took a while, but man, once I got sick of radio talk, my phone got turned off, and I didn't see daylight until I was fully decompressed. Even now, after five hours of grunge, I'm turning on some of the wussiest music the teenage me would kick me in the face for listening to. We have our limits. They may change over time. You may like reading four or five people a day, and then, after a few years, you change your schedule completely. Just stay in tune to how you're feeling after a reading and how the readings go, and you will figure it out.

A Note from Erik from Holbrook

Throughout life, I have found more connections and friendships through the love of music than anything else— probably because, if you love music, then you love to listen, be it stories, music tones, the sound of the human voice, the intensity of a message delivered, and most importantly, the connection.

This is one of many music connections that have stayed with me for years. In the winter of 1993, standing in the hallway of Sachem South before homeroom, the question was asked by someone I consider a rock and roll mentor, Brian Orlando. He always knew not only what was good, but what would suit your own musical tastes, and how you would process it, especially if you 'd never heard it before.

I can hear his question like it was yesterday: "Hey, you ever listened to the alternate lyrics version of 'Don't Cry' on Illusion II?

At this time, I was hellbent, all-in, with Use Your Illusion I. The cassette tape had been abused by over-play in my Walkman to the point that the audio was fading.

I replied, "I heard it, maybe once or twice, but it sounds so downbeat."

And that was the moment Brian explained the depth of the song, the history of it being one of the first ever written by Guns N 'Roses, the difference that time makes from the original lyrics—as the first reaction and premature emotion to a break- up—versus the alternate lyrics, that show a passing of time and more depth to what happened with Izzy. This version was an example of the process of moving on in a break-up and the state of mind afterwards. And of course, the overall blues feel and tone on *Illusion II*, and understanding the blue color scheme in the artwork.

Brian had opened a door, a new connection, letting others into what he found—but also what he felt and wanted to share. I never forgot that. I was so awe-struck by his description, grateful for his insight, and now excited for being "in the know" and wanting to listen to it with this new point of view. I couldn't wait to get home and re-listen to "Don't Cry" until I felt those lyrics and sounds.

To this day, I listen to *Use Your Illusion II* more than the first volume because of this conversation. We've had countless conversations through the years and had many musical connections, from the AC/DC *Live* album to Rob Halford's *Fight*, *Kiss's Alive III*, and even how we all felt when "Headbangers Ball" ended abruptly.

There's always a story behind the song—be it a cover, alternate lyrics, unreleased B-side, hidden tracks, uncredited musician, or the depth of the story portrayed. You name it, if they're mentioning it to you, it's to know if you're on "the level." And that's the connection, the moment both people's eyes light up, and you share the synchronized nod. Yup, they know, and the connection spirals into a shared moment of music, ideas, and interests.

Thank you, Brian, for that connection and for what it meant to be on "the level."

How Did Music Connect You to What You Have Now?

It's been a very black-and-white journey for me when it comes to music. I've loved it since I was a baby, became obsessed with it as a young child, and wanted to do nothing but music once junior high started. The only obstacle I faced was a lack of obvious talent to become a musician. I picked up a guitar once, but the intro to Guns N 'Roses' "Sweet Child O 'Mine" didn't play on its own, and I got pissed. Nobody told me that you had to practice playing the fucking thing. So, even though it took me a while to figure out this loophole of doing music with a rock radio career, I still took a pretty straightforward path. Love music, can't live without music, so use music to earn a paycheck, create friendships, make connections, and open doorways that would otherwise remain closed.

It's easy for me to see how music has connected me to so much, but as free as a bird as I am with rock and roll, how about you? Take a look around you right now. What can you thank music for?

My parents met at a doo-wop concert in 1975. About 2,000 people, with 2,000 different stories, took 2,000 different ways to the same club to see one band sing the same songs. Two of those stories wound up blending into one another for a few chapters, and a spinoff was created in 1978.

In the '80s, you didn't have Facebook to stay connected with friends once your parents decided to leave town and start somewhere new. You didn't have your own phone to shoot the old crew a text when you were feeling lonely in your new town.

You called everyone on your parents' landline and hoped their parents stuck your message to the fridge on a Post-it note. If the note fell to the floor and got brushed under the fridge by the cat, you were soon forgotten about, and that was that. You were wondered about, rumored to be dead, and then everyone moved on.

I never really thought about that until I got into radio in my mid-twenties. My mother moved me out of the Patchogue-Medford School District in 1991. I wasn't yet thirteen. Life truly began for me in a town called Ronkonkoma, so when I talk about my memories, they usually come from my time going to Sachem High School. Those kids in Patchogue-Medford? I forgot about them. Until I started getting phone calls during my morning show. Some of the last names really sounded familiar as I took down their winner info.

One particular Monday morning, I was taking opinions about a song we debuted on 94.3 The Shark a few minutes prior. My intentions were selfish as fuck, because I had written the lyrics to this song, and my much more talented friends recorded it. The message of the song was that, with music, you are never alone. After a few positive phone calls, a shy-sounding gentleman entered the conversation.

"Hi, The Shark, who's this?"

"This is Mike from Patchogue."

"Mike, what's up brother? What did you think of 'Choose Song'?"

"I was wondering if I could get a copy. I'm still crying, brother. I'm a U.S. Army vet, and sometimes I feel like no one understands what I'm going through. That song just made me feel like someone's listening."

Calls like this you never forget. Calls like this are why you still get up at 3 a.m. to do a morning show.

"Mike, first thing I wanna say is thank you for everything you did for me, and thank you for representing Long Island with your service, brother. Can I hook you up with a restaurant gift card?"

"Ah, you don't have to do that, Orlando."

"Cool. What's your last name, brother?"

"Oh ... Correlli. Michael Correlli."

"Correlli? Were you a tall, skinny, blonde-haired kid who fought a guy named Kevin in music class?"

"Ha-ha, I still am. I wasn't sure if you'd remember me, Brian. You mentioned being bullied in Patchogue before you played the song, and I put it together. I've been listening to you for years. How are you?"

Just recently, I got to announce the birth of Mike's granddaughter. Two kids who parted ways thirty years earlier, who took two completely different roads in life, were brought back together simply because they love the same music. Two kids who wouldn't have entered each other's thoughts if they were paid to name childhood friends. Thanks to the power of a single song, we were instantly reminded of each other.

I often get asked why I do so much work with suicide prevention. "Choose Song" was a campaign, but we all do our best to promote mental health awareness every day. The truth is, I tried taking my own life when I was fifteen. It wasn't a very smart move, but it's true, and I don't hide from it. I've mentioned a few times during our ride together in this book that my upbringing wasn't exactly traditional. Truthfully, it sucked. It was loud and bitter and violent. The only thing I was ever encouraged to do was take blame and fuck off. That led to some awful battles with my weight, as I suffered from horrible body-image issues. I dealt with anorexia, bulimia, and the kinds of self-destruction usually associated with teenage girls during "very special" episodes of '90s teen sitcoms. Working out became the one thing I could control, and even though my discipline wasn't the greatest, I could always count on a school gym workout to shake me out of a funk.

Well, one night, things got bad at the house, and I was told I ruined everyone's life by existing. It was 7 p.m. I was two years away from even being eligible for a driver's license, but it didn't matter because school closed at 4 p.m. So, I grabbed my

Walkman, my favorite cassette tape, and just started running through the streets of Ronkonkoma. For a few moments, I was back in control and felt empowered. Things were getting better ... then my tape snapped. My favorite tape, with my favorite songs on it. The only fucking thing that kept me sane was broken, with no way to replace it. I was done. I was done, and I wasn't gonna be stopped.

At that point, on the side of Lake Shore Road, I decided I was done with this life, and I was gonna end it before it could get any worse. At my feet was a broken beer bottle. Perfect. The edges looked sharp. I picked it up and power-walked down to the polluted, disgusting lake where this pathetic excuse for a life was gonna end. I can still remember the feeling of the sand through my toes. I had taken my shoes and socks off to make my exit as comfortable as possible. The glass started cutting into my forearm. Tears were streaming down my face. It wasn't the pain causing them, but the frustration over letting the world get me to this point. *Fuck it,* I thought. *Just press harder and you won't have to think about this anymore.*

Then I heard it. I heard it clear as day. No, it wasn't the voice of my guardian angel speaking down divinely from the heavens to stop me from committing this mortal sin. It was the sound of my favorite singer, singing my favorite song, coming from the boom box of a couple that was divinely sitting on a blanket about a thousand feet away from me. Hearing that one familiar voice, I instantly snapped back to reality. I didn't wanna die anymore. I just wanted to figure out a way to hear my favorite song again. So I wiped the blood with my hoodie, shook the tears off of my face like some tough guy, and walked home.

There was this little radio I kept under my bed. I dragged it out and plugged it in. Everyone was sleeping at this point, so I grabbed the phone and called into a local rock station. The DJ instantly heard the distress in my voice and asked if I was okay. All I remember telling that guy was that it'd been a really rough day—one that was capped off with the cassette copy of my favorite album breaking. A few minutes later, he was playing my favorite song off that album. I cried a bit, fell asleep, and woke up ready to fight another day.

That DJ was Captain Kevin McPartland. He probably saved my life that night. I'm not sure if that was the night I realized I wanted to be a DJ, but it was the night I knew I wanted to help other people who were struggling with the will to carry on. Years later, Kevin and I became co-workers and friends, and it was never lost on me that this guy had such a major impact on my life.

The album I was so upset to lose was the debut Candlebox album. I know, I know, these fucking guys again. Hear me out. Their music hit me hard ever since they came out in 1993. There were many other incidents where the thought of ending it all could have entered my head, but their music was always a big reason why it didn't. Kevin Martin's lyrics just always made me feel like someone understood me, and that's all I needed to get through the worst of it.

By 2013, I was fully immersed in my career as a morning-show host. Kevin and I had become pretty tight by that point from working together at different shows. He and I were on the phone one day discussing an upcoming show and talking about how we could get the band in the studio to promote it, when something truly profound hit me upside the head. I was walking through my hometown, where I still live, while talking to Kevin, because why not? I might as well get my hike in while I'm working. Kevin was thanking me for always helping the band. At this moment, I didn't have the chance to stop him and tell him that I owed him more than I could ever pay back, because my shoe became untied. As I crouched down to fix the situation, while listening to his appreciation of me, I realized where I was. Almost the exact same spot I was standing twenty years earlier when my tape snapped. Same block. Same corner.

The song that my junior-high-school friend called in to request is called "Choose Song." I wrote the lyrics, but Kevin is one of the vocalists who sings those words that encourage people to listen to their favorite music when times get tough: "There's a brighter note tomorrow / Don't choose the end, *choose song.*"

Okay. The story, I swear, is all true—but what the fuck does this have to do with Tarot? Well ... everything. The entire purpose of this book is to connect you to Tarot through music. The entire reason music unifies us so well is because the subject matters contained in some of the greatest rock and roll songs ever written are filled with emotions we all not only relate to, but have *been* through. To know that there is someone in this world who gets what you have been going through is the comfort that can stop you from making an awful choice, and the encouragement to make great ones.

Look at some of the subjects covered in Tarot. Relationship issues. Communication breakdowns. Paranoid delusions. Anxiety. Isolation. Writing about these very things got more than a few bands into the Rock & Roll Hall of Fame. There may not be a "Tarot Hall of Fame," but you probably know a few rock star Tarot card readers. They're good because they understand these things. They don't simply talk to you about it. They feel it. They prove to you that they feel it. When you refer someone to a therapist, it's usually because they understand you. The same is said about great psychics. They've really understood what I was going through and offered some great advice.

Your favorite songs still get played by you because they still speak to you. We're all connected. Tarot is just one of many things that reminds us of that. It just so happens that Tarot and rock and roll are two of the best ways to remind us of that.

A Note from Brian Vander Ark, The Verve Pipe

I've always believed that, besides our physical form as a human species, music is our lowest common denominator. We all enjoy music in some capacity, from the child in Mumbai to the CEO in Manhattan. It's the one art form that has an importance that we can all agree upon. And, though personal taste in music can unite or divide us, the fact that there are seemingly endless genres and sub-genres means that we may find some common ground there as well.

Run-D.M.C. hooked up with Aerosmith, and suddenly I find myself buying Raising Hell. *Born and raised in Dutch Christian Reformed Church, I never would have considered South African street music to be of my liking. Enter Paul Simon, and I'm absolutely stunned by the beautiful* Graceland.

But some things are constant. A favorite comfort food, a familiar go-to. And the curator is a radio personality who you may never have had a connection with, other than over the airwaves, amidst the din of terrestrial radio stations that clutter your mind. And then you meet him, and you find a true connection. That's Brian Anthony (Orlando) at 94.3 The Shark.

I don't know a band that doesn't know him, hasn't sat in on an interview with him, hasn't been captivated by that baritone voice, flexed as strong and mighty as his biceps. His veracious love and knowledge of music transcends the dead air of most interviews. He's an interviewee's dream; he can be directed into the subjects you want to discuss, because he listens. I was honored when he asked me to write the lyrics from my song 'The Freshmen" on the back of his hand so he could have it permanently tattooed. My hand was shaking, my mind second-guessing the spelling of "merely" in "We were merely freshmen."

My band, The Verve Pipe, has visited the station many times since. We have the shared vision, not only of a custodian of music we love, but also one we can trust. His word-of-mouth recommendations—Have you heard so and so yet? If you like that song, you should check out the live version from 2017...etc., etc.

He and I do not share a connection through physical form; I'm about a foot taller, and due to his bodybuilder's physique, weigh less. The weight we do share, however, is the importance of music in our lives.

Music is But One Connection

The one thing that always blew my mind when I would stand out in front of a sold-out music venue to introduce a band was how we all wound up in the same room together. Take a club the size of The Paramount, in Huntington, NY, which holds about 1,600 people, I believe. That's 1,600 different roads that led everyone into the same room. That's 1,600 different stories that all share at least one page, and perhaps a few chapters. At a concert, we all stand there singing one language, emitting our strongest emotions for this intangible energy force that drives us to work, to the gym, and to a night at a show. That person you're standing next to has no idea who you are, but you share a very powerful bond as you both sing the exact same lines back to your favorite singer. Actually, there is a good chance that's slightly incorrect, as I continue to discover daily that I've been fucking up lyrics to songs for years—but you get my basic premise here, right?

Everyone is a stranger, until they're not. Even our parents. We had nine months of peace before they began screwing us up. Some people, though...some people *feel* different. You know the type of people I'm talking about. The ones that make you feel at home the second you meet them. The ones that make the first time saying 'hello' feel more like, 'Oh, there you are!'

Why do you think that is? Is it just the energy that feels good, or is it something deeper? Is the energy familiar because you have actually felt it before? There is a belief in this world that our souls drive this meat suit we're currently in, and when this body craps out, we will move on to the next until we reach angel status, or black belt, or whatever it is that gets us retired from the earthly plane. The idea is that we all play different roles at different times in each other's lives, so we all learn different lessons.

My grandmother was an extremely overbearing worrywart. She admitted this many times as I got older and once actually said to me, "Bri, I see these kids out on the streets, and I actually say to myself, 'Why couldn't I let Brian do that? Why couldn't I let him play like that instead of worrying so much about him being out?'"

Well, one day, I had an incredible past-life regression from a dear friend, Marcy, from the Port Jeff Salt Cave. During this intense session, it came out that in the early 1600s, my grandmother was actually the mother of my three children, and I decided to up and leave one day out of boredom. I understand how this sounds. I don't completely buy into past lives all of the time either. But the second the words came out of Marcy's mouth, a weight lifted off of me. It's as if decades of frustration and anger just dissipated. At that moment, I could get back to simply missing my grandmother and remembering how important she was to me.

I feel closer to her now than I did before she left this plane in 2019. Without getting into too much detail, it was a very complicated relationship. She loved me, I knew that, but there was a lot of anger. A lot of fear. To think that we knew each other before, and were working out a very complicated history in new roles within a completely different setting, makes every argument, every moment of bitterness, resolve in light of this new information. The one thing that still connects Grandma and me, five years after she passed? The Mets. Those *son-of-a-bitching-god-darn-Mets* that have broken our hearts over and over, while simultaneously giving us thousands of hours to laugh at them.

Now, this is a one-hundred-percent true story. Grandma and I wanted nothing more than to see a Met, *any* Met, throw a no-hitter. They were one of only two teams in MLB to never complete a game without giving up a single hit, and for decades, we watched every game we could so we could finally say it happened. I was alone on June 1, 2012, when Johan Santana finally did it for the Mets on 134 pitches. I can recite the final call in seven languages, and backwards. As tears streamed down my face, my phone exploded with calls, but I wouldn't dare pick up the phone until one name appeared on my phone screen.

"Hey, Grandma."

"Brian, you son of a bitch. Did you see it? Johan did it!!! I can die now. Get over here tomorrow, they're gonna replay it. I'm going to bed now. Goodnight."

So, that's what I did. I drove fifteen miles the next day so we could say we saw it together. To watch Johan Santana throw the first no-hitter in NY Mets history. The night after Grandma passed, it was announced that the Mets would finally have new owners. It took a while to become official, but I knew that the Mets would be a connection that Grandma would use to kick me in the ass when needed.

I had been going through a rough time at work, and my head was lost in the smoke-filled clouds. I lost my wallet—for three fucking days. My fiancé checked the hamper three times. I physically turned the hamper upside down. No wallet. On day four, I was furiously driving to work at 3 a.m. as I worried about renewing and replacing all of my identification, when "Tenth Ave Freeze-Out" and "I Just Called to Say I Love You" came on my 30,000-song playlist, back-to-back. Bruce and Stevie Wonder never played back to back. They were Grandma's two favorite songs. A few hours later, while I was on the air, I got a call that the wallet was found...in the hamper. Okay. I'm relieved now, and exhausted.

When I got home from work, I took my fiancé to a brand-new Mexican place. She asked me how I was feeling. I said—and I still remember—"I know that was Grandma that brought my wallet back, but I wish she could just call me and say, 'That was me, you dummy.'" As the words left my mouth, our waiter came over to introduce myself. "Hi, my name is Johan, and I'll be taking care of you."

I'm crying as I'm writing this. I'm in a fucking coffee shop, and everyone must think I'm nuts. If someone else had a die-hard Mets fan grandparent like I did, they would understand.

To this day, six years after Grandma left this world, the Mets are still our connection. The world is full of them. Tarot is full of them. Those seventy-eight cards don't just represent feelings and situations. They represent connections. You are connecting someone to their feelings to help them in the situations they're seeking guidance in. Use your energy to connect with their energy. Feel the connection. And have a great reading.

Afterword

By Kevin Martin, Candlebox

It 's not often that you meet someone who meets your life in such a profound way, but that 's exactly what happened when Orlando and I crossed paths over a decade ago. Our connection was instant, forged through the shared language of music— Orlando, with his boundless passion as a radio DJ, and me, out on the road as a touring musician, both of us living and breathing the rhythms that defined us.

It wasn't just the sound of the guitar or the beat of the drum—it was the heart of the music that brought us together. We both shared an undeniable love for Seattle 's music scene, and in particular, Mother Love Bone, whose influence still runs deep through everything we do

Over the years, Orlando has been a constant presence, not only as a radio DJ but as a lifeline for so many musicians and fans alike. He 's been the kind of friend you can rely on, no matter what. Through thick and thin, whether it 's been the high of a sold-out show or the lows of navigating the music business, Orlando has been there—steadfast and unwavering, always with a heart full of support. I truly feel blessed to call him a friend.

We walked this wild journey together, and after over ten years of friendship, there 's no one else I 'd rather share these moments with. His authenticity, generosity, and unshakeable love for the music community have made him an integral part of my life, and I'm honored to write this epilogue for a man who's nothing short of a brother to me. This book is a testament to his journey, and I couldn't be prouder to stand beside him as he shares his story with the world.

Thank you, Orlando, for everything. Here's to many more years of music, friendship, and memories.

Which Song Would You Assign?

Major Arcana

0) The Fool

_____

1) The Magician

_____

2) The High Priestess

_____

3) The Empress

_____

4) The Emperor

_____

5) The Hierophant

_____

6) The Lovers

_____

7) The Chariot

_____

8) Strength

_____

9) The Hermit

_____

10) The Wheel of Fortune

_____

11) Justice

_____

12) The Hanged Man

_____

13) Death

_____

14) Temperance

_____

15) The Devil

_____

16) The Tower

_____

17) The Star

_____

18) The Moon

_____

19) The Sun

_____

20) Judgement

_____

21) The World

_____

Minor Arcana

PENTACLES
   Ace

Two

Three

Four

Five

Six

Seven

Eight

_____

Nine

_____

Ten

_____

Page

_____

Knight

_____

Queen

_____

King

_____

WANDS
Ace

_____

Two

_____

Three

_____

Four

_____

Five

_____

Six

_____

Seven

_____

Eight

_____

Nine

_____

Ten

_____

Page

_____

Knight

Queen

King

SWORDS
Ace

Two

Three

Four

Five

Six

Seven

_____

Eight

_____

Nine

_____

Ten

_____

Page

_____

Knight

_____

Queen

_____

King

_____

CUPS
  Ace

_____

Two

_____

Three

_____

Four

_____

Five

_____

Six

_____

Seven

_____

Eight

_____

Nine

_____

Ten

_____

Page

_____

Knight

_____

Queen

_____

King

_____

Acknowledgements

To my soul brother, Chris Lipani:

Emotionally and physically the strongest guy I know. Who would have thought a long overdue night out to catch up and talk about chicks and junior high school gym class would lead us into this crazy metaphysical world at EXACTLY the same time after thirty years. I have only gotten this far on this journey because you had faith in your crazy old Ronkonkoma friend. I love you, brother.

To Rocky Robilotto and Mike Loper:

Losing you at a young age was a hard lesson to learn. Realizing I never did lose you was one of my greatest. Thank you for looking down and checking in, for watching over me, and helping me get out of too many jams to count ... or admit. I think about you both every day.

Miss you, baby.

To Snake Sabo, Kevin Martin, Vinnie Dombroski, John Hampson, and Brian Vander Ark:

Thank you for the music that led me through the darkness and played even louder during celebrations. To think some punk kid with an stack of eclectically selected mixed CDs would one day not only get to thank his heroes, and not only work with his heroes, but also call them trusted friends is a testament to how powerful this crazy universe is. Thank you for believing in me, for trusting me, and for being such an integral part of so many chapters of my life.

To my father, John:

It may not have been perfect. It may not have always been great. But I never once forgot the many lessons you taught me about manners, respect, and communication. This book doesn't get written if not for many hours of taking me to Record World to picking out my five 45s for a dollar and then explaining as much as you could about each band.

To Aunt Leslie and Uncle Richie:

There is so much I can say, but the six thousand Bruce references in this book are just one example of the influence and impact you had on me. Thank you for showing me so much art and music that it became a cornerstone of my morning show radio content.

To Aunt Donna and Uncle Tom:

The nurturing aunt and uncle. The wise ones. The ones who showed me so much love and support despite being just a liiiiiittttle bit different than everyone else in the family. For the memories and the pictures and, most importantly, the smiles and the belief in me, thank you.

To my grandmothers, Grace and Jean:

I wouldn't be half the man I am today without either of you. There is no love like a grandmother's love and I was lucky to have two very unique and strong-willed women to show me how to be the same. You are legends, and I hope that one day someone thinks back and appreciates having me in their life the way I appreciate both of you, my angels looking down.

To my mom, Diane:

Okay. Go ahead. Say it. I told you so. There isn't a person mentioned in this book who is more responsible for the spiritual and metaphysical side of it than you. Watching you read cards all of these years was just one lesson. Watching you deal with skeptics and those who became obsessed taught me things I can only hope will be half as educational throughout this book. Your education in this stuff cannot be measured in money or explained in words. Thank you!

To 943 The Shark:

You took a chance on me back on 9-22-2014. I am sure you regret it quite a bit, but I commend your patience and will forever be grateful for the opportunities, as this book shows.

To Nicole:

For your ideas, love, support and dedication to being with me as each new chapter unfolds, I am forever thankful, forever grateful, and always in appreciation. You never stop coming up with ways to push me further, and raise me higher. Your love, trust, and faith in me has carried me through the hardest parts of my journey.

To my listeners throughout twenty years of rock radio, from Atlantic City, NY, through Westchester, and back home to Long Island, NY:

Thank you. Thank you for trusting me to be a part of your ride every day. Thank you for believing that I'm worth your time. Thank you for keeping me in the passenger seat for two decades. Let's all enjoy this ride together!

About the Author

Brian Orlando is a second generation tarot card reader, first generation psychic medium, and twenty-year rock radio music veteran. Brian's love for music began in his uncle's basement apartment. As a toddler he was able to tell what songs on *Meet The Beatles* were skipped, and hurried back up to tell his parents.

While music was an obvious love, the world of tarot took decades for him to appreciate, having grown up with a psychic mother. No rebellious teen was going to listen, and only after working with various psychics during his eleven years as a morning drive radio host did Brian finally start to embrace his gifts. Uniting his first love with what has revealed itself as his true calling, Brian has combined his passions with his expertise and experiences to present a teaching style designed to empower, educate, and entertain the living heck out of you.

Connect with Brian on Instagram at @Orlando0616 or visit his website rocknsoultarot.net.